The Book of Family Fun

The Book
of Family Fun

The Book of Family Fun *is not affiliated with* FamilyFun *magazine,
a title of Disney Magazine Publishing, Inc.*

A Barbour Book

ISBN   1-55748-653-0

 Member of the
Evangelical Christian
Publishers Association

Published by   Barbour and Company, Inc.
                P.O. Box 719
                Uhrichsville, Ohio 44683

Printed in the United States of America

Contents

Introduction

There are two words missing from the title of this book. Oh, it makes sense the way it reads, but the title doesn't say exactly what is conveyed between the covers. The two words are *Christ-centered.*

Children are truly a gift from God, the fulfillment of our wishes and dreams for a family. If we are to be the kind of parents God desires—the kind that commits "their house" to the Lord—all our family activities will reflect that single-minded devotion to Jesus Christ. But that doesn't mean for a minute that fun takes a back seat!

The Book of Family Fun is a year-round resource for your family. Whether indoors or al fresco, at home or four for the road, celebrating Christ's birth, or remembering the beginning of a special family member, you'll find ideas for making the moments of your family's life memorable, meaningful, and FUN, without ruining your budget.

All the activities presented in *The Book of Family Fun* are favorites of our contributors and editors and, as with so many other kinds of child- rearing techniques, many have been traded from one parent to another. Some have even been handed down—surely the highest recommendation—from children to grandchildren!

The greatest gift a parent can give a child is a loving, joy-filled, Christian home. *The* "Christ-centered" *Book Family Fun* is one of many resources to be used toward that end.

THE PUBLISHER

The Book of Family Fun

The Book of Family Fun

indoors

———

**God has provided us with shelter. . .
and the gift of imagination.**

———

Grabbing This Moment's Joy

by Sandra Picklesimer Aldrich

Proverbs 17:22 (NIV) tells us that "a cheerful heart is good medicine, but a crushed spirit dries up the bones." But even knowing this truth, it seemed to take forever after my husband died before I could laugh again.

But laughter did return. And I remember when it happened. One of my relatives was giving an account of his zany experiences. I've long forgotten the story he told, but I recall that the corners of my mouth turned up as I listened. In that moment, I made a conscious decision to give in to a rib-splitting laugh. And it felt good.

Since then I've learned the scientific reason for that feeling of well-being: Endorphins—a form of the body's own medicine—are released from the brain when we laugh.

I've also learned that not only does laughter relieve daily tension, but it creates marvelous memories, for us as well as for our youngsters.

Laura's children were four and three when their dad took off. Laughing was the last thing Laura wanted to do, but she also knew she couldn't sit in a darkened house and expect the children to be quiet, too. One evening, in desperation, she draped a blanket over a card table and suggested the children play "Indian."

Within a few minutes, the four year old peeked from under the table and gestured for Laura to join them.

She opened her mouth to say "No," but instead said, "Sure!" and thoroughly enjoyed the silly moments with her little ones. The cheeriness of their time together was indeed "good medicine" for all of them.

Peggy's week in her blue-suit office world had been rough. Now Saturday's chores loomed; it was raining and both her kids had colds. She pulled on her sweat shirt, then noticed she had it on backward. She sighed and started to turn the logo to the front. Suddenly she grinned at her mirrored reflection and turned her sweat pants inside out before she tugged them on. Then she pulled her hair into a top knot and tied it with a pair of her daughter's lavender tights.

Not only did she feel appropriately dressed for the gloomy morning, but she still occasionally gives in to other tension-relieving "weird days," much to the delight of her family.

As my children and I were learning to have fun together, we found that the unplanned events—the trips to the cider mills or impromptu garbage-bag tobogganing—were the ones that gave us the greatest pleasure, not the trips we overplanned for weeks.

We even started looking for the joy in each moment, expecting to be surprised by the unexpected. Once, we took bread to a local pond, planning to feed the geese. But as we tossed the first pieces toward the graceful birds, the water suddenly churned with hundreds of greedy carp snatching the crumbs beneath the reaching beaks! We were so delighted to see the pond come alive that we laughed repeatedly as we tossed in more bread.

Our journey toward renewed laughter has been arduous at times, but we've learned to grab this moment. Along the way, we've discovered hearts ready for adventure, and fun.

Sandra P. Aldrich is the Dean of Students for the Focus on the Family Institute for Family Studies in Colorado Springs, Colorado.

Adapted from **From One Single Mother to Another** *by Sandra P. Aldrich. Copyright © 1991, Regal Books, Ventura, Calif. 93003. Used by permission.*

Start Your Day Right

Family devotions are always a good idea but may be impossible to schedule. One solution is to have them in the morning before breakfast, and limit the time to five minutes...that way you'll always have time!

Begin with a Bible verse or read a pertinent family devotional. Or, write out Bible verses ahead of time, place them in a jar, and have family members take turns drawing a verse and reading it aloud.

Another idea is to say prayers that relate to the activities of the day ahead. If a child has a test that day, pray for him or her to do the best job possible. Have a silent moment when personal, individual requests are shared with our Heavenly Father.

Your day will go much better if you start it off—as a family—with the Lord.

Adapted from **The Big Book of Family Fun** *by Claudia Arp and Linda Dillow (Thomas Nelson Publishers, 1994). Used with permission by the publisher.*

Share More than a Meal

Family fellowship and sharing are important to our family. Here are some ideas we have used to promote this.

We start the day with a devotional from the book *Train up a Child* by Jean Ahern Lubin. This book provides interactive devotions that are fun for many ages. At dinner we use other special ways to promote communication and love within our family. The first thing we do is to go around the dinner table and give each person the chance to tell about their day. Nobody is allowed to interrupt! In addition, we use two printed resources. The first is *Kid's Choices* published by Rainfall that are cards on which are printed different, real-life dilemmas. Children are asked what they would do in different situations and how they feel about certain things. Biblical principles are applied to everyday situations. The second resource is the *Bright Ideas Calendar of 365 Self-concept Activities* published by McDonald Pub. The activity for each day is designed to help children learn about themselves and their relationship with the world and the people around them.

Finally, as a special treat, we have adapted an Emilie Barnes seminar idea for Sunday mealtime. Emily is a well-known Christian speaker and suggests the use of special clip candles that can be placed on dinner plates. While she suggested their use at the Christmas holiday, we have adapted their use as a special treat at dinner. Each person goes around the table and says "I give you my light" until all the candles are lit. The children think this is pretty special and they remind us to get out the candles even before dinner is prepared.

Valerie and Bradford Smith
Apple Valley, California

Devotionals Made Easy

For years we struggled with trying to have a daily devotional time with our children. One of our problems was a lack of material available for our little ones. We started using their Sunday school take-home papers on some evenings. The Bible stories and life applications are geared to their ages and reinforce what they learned in Sunday school as well!

Terry L. Pfleghaar
Elk River, Minnesota

A Walk through the Bible

Devotions with kids can come to life by tapping into their natural curiosity about the world. For instance, if you're reading from Paul's letters, trace his missionary journeys with the help of a Bible atlas (there are many from which to choose). By using such a resource, settings and cultures become much more real and Bible stories are firmly planted in the children's minds.

Trace the journey of Abraham as he followed God's leading...the Hebrews from Egypt to the Promised Land...the footsteps of Jesus Christ from Nazareth to Calvary. The possibilities for enlightened study are at your fingertips (and local Christian bookstore).

Another suggestion is to create a worship center with objects pertinent to your current devotions. For example, if you're studying Paul's journeys, include seashells, miniature tents, heavy rope from a make-believe ship, as well as rough-hewn crosses on a makeshift altar. After the devotion, which is held sitting around the altar, close with a few favorite hymns and prayer.

Hannah Wilkinson
Harrington Park, New Jersey

Summer Bible Club

When my daughter was five, she announced that she knew the whole Bible! After further questioning, I realized she was bored with the same old Sunday school stories and needed more challenging material.

A six-week Summer Bible Club was started at our apartment for our daughters and some of their friends. Meeting for almost two hours in the morning, we painted shells, made salt and flour creations, and sewed sock puppets. Each week we learned about a different woman in the Bible (only girls attended). The format was simple: Bible story, memory verse, singing, one craft.

The Summer Bible Club was kicked off with an ice cream sundae party and ended with silly water games based around our wading pool. A great way to share the Bible and have fun!

Janet M. Bair
Ansonia, Connecticut

Care Coupons

Share some tender, loving care through care coupons. They are encouraging, fun, and self-esteem builders. Simply fill out index cards with expressions of how you will care for one another. We have received (and given) such coupons as one free backrub; one task of your choice completed; one chapter of your favorite book read to you; and so on.

The choices are innumerable and the "care" comes through, loud and clear.

Kathryn Bechtel
Muncy Valley, Pennsylvania

What to Do

Want to spend some time together as a family but are at a loss as to what to do? Here's a suggestion.

Find a large container, such as a box, and have each member of the family write down on separate pieces of paper what things he or she would like the family to do together. The suggestions could range from taking a day trip into the country to staying home and playing a game. Other ideas include: seeing a movie; going rollerblading; seeing what's new in camping at an RV show; making a bed for that special doll or a bird feeder for the yard (see p. 105-106).

Each suggestion should be signed so that the activites can be chosen on a rotating basis to make sure that each family member has an equal number of turns. An important point is that all should agree up front to partake in the activity; that way everyone learns to appreciate each other's feelings as well as experience new things.

When an activity is chosen, another suggestion should be put into the box by the person whose activity was selected.

The Fun Jar

Our family of seven has a Fun Jar, and it can make things happen.

We took an old jar and decorated it and now we use it to save money for going places the whole family enjoys. The money comes from pop or soda cans we find, extra change, coins we find, and a little part of the money we get for gifts. We watch the money grow until there is enough for the activity we have chosen.

For instance, it took seven months to save enough to go to the local amusement park. Sometimes we'll use the funds to go out for pizza, rent a movie, or play a game of miniature golf.

We enjoy the pride the children have knowing they made it happen.

The Parker Family
Holton, Michigan

"And the Winner Is..."

Every year, perhaps in the summer, take time out to plan an awards night for your family. Beforehand, decide on the categories for the awards, such as Most Helpful, Most Considerate, Best Smiler, Miss (or Mr.) Sunshine, Best Picker-Upper, and so on until there is an award honoring an admirable quality or trait of each family member.

Make a trophy for each by cutting a tall, narrow box to the desired shape, topping it with a star or appropriate statue, and then covering it with aluminum foil. The ceremony could be its own event or it could be part of another family gathering such as a special dinner. The important thing is that each person is recognized and made to feel part of a winning team, your family.

Family Fun Night

At first you may want to make this a once-a-month evening and then graduate to once-a-week (or vice versa). Don't overstructure the activities (no one wants to be in school all day) and be sure to be flexible. If no one but you wants to do a certain activity, choose something else.

Some starters: Plan an international meal, or have each family member concoct their own dish to share. Switch places at the dinner table and see how others see you! Follow dinner (everyone cleans up!) with a family concert, treasure hunt, game night, or family conference on a topic that interests most members (finances, genealogy, travel, and so on).

If you make it fun, they will come!

Adapted from The Big Book of Family Fun *by Claudia Arp and Linda Dillow (Thomas Nelson Publishers, 1994). Used with permission by the publisher.*

Plan a Fun Night

Choose one night each week to set aside for family fun. Plan the activities according to the season and the ages of your children. Pop some popcorn; play a board game; borrow a video from the library or a Christian bookstore; take a walk together or go for a bike ride. Don't forget to ask your children for suggestions; sometimes all they want to do is to cuddle up with Mom or Dad and have a good book read to them.

Kathryn Bechtel
Muncy Valley, Pennsylvania

Memorable Evenings

Basically, a family night is anything at all that we as a family do together. Some wonderful memories have come from evenings such as these.

We have walked down to the corner store and bought doughnuts and brought them back home...all in the rain.

Even Mom and Dad played hide and seek one evening in the house.

Once a month a night is set aside as "date night." One parent takes one child out and the other parent takes another for a time of one-on-one interaction. When our daughter was fifteen Dad took her on her first official date. He knocked on the front door to pick her up. He hoped to serve as a role model for how a real date should treat her.

We made cookies and decorated them together.

Our family learned something new together. We have taken music, crafts, and dancing lessons.

A game of badminton is great fun, especially when followed by homemade milkshakes.

We have ordered pizza at midnight!

Speaking of pizza, we have also taken pizza to a park and then everyone found a swing.

We have made greeting cards and sent them to a sick relative. Instead of sending them all at once, we mailed one a day.

When it's snowing, we have taken walks just to watch the falling flakes.

D. Eldridge
Kokomo, Indiana

Simple Things

Family fun doesn't have to be a meticulously scheduled, every-detail-planned activity. Here are some impromptu activities that work wonders at keeping the lines of communication open between parent and child:

A cookie break. Don't just bake cookies; sit down and eat them together.

A game of Double Solitaire.

Listening to music or watching a TV program of your child's choice.

Making a collage of items from your kitchen—cereal, pasta, beans.

Adapted from The Big Book of Family Fun *by Claudia Arp and Linda Dillow (Thomas Nelson Publishers, 1994). Used with permission by the publisher.*

Come One, Come All

When we have Family Night we may invite all family members, some of whom don't live with us, and everyone brings a prepared dish. Sometimes we'll precook and freeze certain meals and have fun just cooking together. After eating, we play games or watch videos. It's just fun being together.

Sandy Umber
Springdale, Arkansas

Take Turns

Each member of the family takes a turn being in charge of the planning of our Family Fun Night. This person chooses the meal, leads the prayer, plans the activities, picks out the bedtime story, and concludes the night with prayer. You'd be surprised how much a two or three year old is capable of doing if given the opportunity!

The Umlauf Family
Wausau, Wisconsin

All Together

Friday night is Family Fun Night at our house. In fact, the fun starts directly after school for our only child. She is allowed to watch one extra television show than on other days. Dinner is also her choice, and that is always a fun decision. After the "fun" portion of the evening, she gets to sleep in our room. My husband sets up a blanket tent and my daughter camps out under it with her sleeping bag. It's no wonder that she looks forward to Friday all week!

Cheryl Burney
Royal Oak, Michigan

Our Family's Favorite

A favorite evening for our family is to spread out in the living room on a blanket, pop some popcorn, and watch a video. Since we do not have cable, I have given my mother some empty videotapes and from time to time she tapes movies and shows for us to enjoy. This way we save money on renting movies.

If it's cold outside, we build a fire in the fireplace and have hot chocolate with our popcorn. If it's warm, we substitute milkshakes.

Kimberly Wentworth
Colbert, Georgia

Lights, Camera, Action!

On one Family Fun Night we had "Jungle Book Night." We watched the Walt Disney movie, ate food that one might find in the jungle (like coconut), and acted out parts of the movie. The best part was seeing Mom, Dad, and the kids dressed up in little grass skirts. The skirts were made of newsprint and everyone enjoyed making them. The total cost of this unusual evening was less than three dollars! We have had similar fun nights acting out "Lady and the Tramp" and "The Little Mermaid."

Denise Johnson
Fairgrove, Michigan

Pizza's Here!

Friday night is Family Fun Night and here's what makes it special. Dad and the kids make their own pizza together while Mom sets up the family room for the fun. Our children are not allowed to watch television very often, so watching one movie a week while we eat pizza is a real treat.

Sally Lind
Gibsonia, Pennsylvania

Let Loose in the Library

A fun, free evening for the entire family can be had at the local library. At many libraries you can rent family videos at no charge. You can also check out CDs and cassettes and often you can listen to these in one of the library's sound rooms. For older children it's fun to have a contest to see who can find a specific book first, using the library computer. Kids soon become familiar with how the library system works.

Stefanie Harris
Phoenix, Arizona

A Worthy Watch

On Family Fun Night, we go to a Christian bookstore and rent a great family movie for all of us to watch.

Melissa Dillman
Middleburg, Pennsylvania

Share the Love

Does it seem more and more like you are living in a house full of strangers? Since my husband and I both work, we spend many evenings collapsed in front of the television set, exhausted. Reconnect and get those family feelings back with Family Night, held every Tuesday at our home.

A favorite activity is to check the local newspaper and attend a fundraiser dinner being held at a local church or for a civic group. For example, every February we enjoy the Firemen's Chili Supper!

You'll feel the love you have for each other...and then you'll be able to share that love with others.

Mary Girshner
Rogers, Arkansas

Give unto Others

Every Tuesday evening my family visits a local nursing home. While this may not sound like fun to most, the joy in my children's faces at giving something of themselves is a wonderful sight. We play games with those who are able, give gentle backrubs, pass out homemade cookies, and ask the residents about their childhood. On the way home we usually stop for an ice cream cone to top off a rewarding evening.

Robin Swentek
Frederic, Wisconsin

Saturday Morning with Dad

My husband and daughter have made a commitment to spend every Saturday morning together. They have breakfast together—an economical meal to eat out—and then have time for a fun activity, and time to accomplish weekend chores and projects. Right now they enjoy cinnamon toast, or they may go to a fast-food or family restaurant. Someday, when our daughter is older, they may try a fine dining experience!

In a larger family, a special time once once a month with each child would still be special.

The Sweet Family
Huntsburg, Ohio

Who Is that Mystery Person?

A simple game for the whole family to play involves guessing the identity of a mystery member of the family.

You could play this game like "twenty questions" and have one person think of an individual and then answer the family's questions with only yes or no. At the end of twenty questions, the one answering provides the person's identity. If someone guesses correctly, he or she thinks of the next person.

Mike Froio
Rome, New York

A Time for Reading

In this fast-paced age it is sometimes hard for everyone in the family to connect. Reading good Christian books out loud together is one way to have fun and be together.

Find a comfortable spot in the living room (couch, floor, or whatever) and have one person volunteer to read from a chosen book. Many children do not like to read on their own and this time of listening and reading expands their—and everyone's—horizons. (Even Dad enjoys these times.)

Susan J. Colwell
Windsor, New York

Once upon a Time...

This activity will appeal to parents of younger children from pre-school to second or third grades.

Begin by sitting in a circle and listing favorite stories that everyone knows. (Examples might include "The Three Little Pigs," "Goldilocks and the Three Bears," "The Three Billy Goats Gruff," "Aladdin," and so on.) One parent then begins telling what seems to be a familiar story but goes strangely awry. At that point the child sitting next to the first storyteller continues the story and so it goes around the circle until at the end the story is unlike any anyone has ever heard! Each person's story should not last too long (parents may have to intervene). Ideally, the parent who began the story should finish it, hopefully with a very exciting and happy ending.

If the children are still interested, let someone else begin another "fractured fable" and watch the silliness erupt. If someone has a video camera, these story times are great for filming.

Hannah Wilkinson
Harrington Park, New Jersey

The Benefits of Board Games

Our family will plan one Saturday when we and our three daughters will play educational and fun board games all day long. We serve easy meals (cereal, soup and sandwiches) and try to have few routine responsibilities.

Sometimes we feel the need to play games one on one, one parent and one child. At these times, I ask special questions, such as "How am I doing as a mom?" or "What would you change about me and how I deal with you if you could change anything?" The answers are always significant.

Tama Carter
Palm Bay, Florida

How Do You Play Henopoly?

Because our family loves to play board games, for Christmas we made up our own game—called "Henopoly," from our last name—and gave it to the kids. Unlike Monopoly, Henopoly involves things kids relate to, such as allowance, chores, and everyday activities, while stressing Christian principles. Here's how the game works.

You'll need some play money—dollars and coins—for the bank. Since we are not too artistic, we chose to use a program we had on our computer to print the game squares. There are four main corner squares: Start (collect $3 allowance); Give to the church; Play with fire (lose half of all money); and Savings (deposit 10 percent of cash on hand). There are six squares between each corner. For these you might include Didn't make bed, pay 38 cents; Didn't feed dog, pay 17 cents; Shovel snow, collect 57 cents; Help each other, collect $2.25; Visit an elderly neighbor, collect $5.00; Take dance lessons, pay $12.00; Swim alone, lose turn; Say your memory verse, roll again; and so on.

All players begin with $20 in cash and $30 in a savings book. You must donate at least 10 percent of money you received going around the board one time every time you pass the church. This money is placed in the center of the board; if someone goes broke, they may go to the church to borrow money, but only for necessities.

Every time a player passes the savings spot you must deposit at least 10 percent of cash on hand. When a player passes Start, he or she collects 10 percent interest on savings book and also $3.00

allowance. Children will soon understand that money at home in the piggy bank doesn't gain interest like it will in a savings account. Only one die is used when we play the game.

You can play this game with any age group, but you should adjust the amount and board items to the ages playing. The biggest lesson to be learned? Money doesn't grow on trees!

The Henshue Family
Saylorsburg, Pennsylvania

When is a Rook a Radish?

Our family enjoys the game of chess, a game kids of all ages can learn to play. One way to make it fun is to make all the chess pieces edible...hence, a rook just might be a radish!

Cover a chess (checkers) board with plastic wrap and then use your imagination with what you've got in the refrigerator. We use grapes for pawns, strawberries with a toothpick inserted in top for bishops or knights, a stately piece of cheddar with toothpick for the queen, and the king...well, a small chocolate bar is such sweet victory.

Judith Cooper
New York, New York

Play Bible Trivial

Our family likes to make up and play games of Bible trivia. We adjust the questions according to the age level of the players. Players can be divided into teams or compete individually. While we keep a tally of points, those who do the least well often need the most encouragement. Thus, we award prizes of Christian books, stickers, and posters to all participants.

Pat Harms
Marengo, Illinois

It's Quiz Time!

When we're sitting around the house with nothing to do, I get out our Bible quiz book and ask questions. It's fun to see who knows what about the Bible and to learn the things we don't know.

Audrey Anderson
Winnsboro, Louisiana

Here are two Bible trivia resources that may aid you in making up your own game. The Fun Book of Bible Trivia, Books 1 and 2, by Robyn Martins (Barbour and Company, Inc.) are filled with word games, quizzes, word searches, and fill-in-the-blanks.

Bible Hide-and-Seek

Here's a way to memorize the Bible and play a game at the same time.

Write a Bible verse on a piece of paper and then choose one family member to be "It." After the others have left the room and are counting to twenty-five, "It" hides the verse. Whoever finds the verse receives 100 points.

When the verse is found, the discoverer reads it aloud and then everyone says it together. When the verse is committed to memory, another person is chosen to be "It."

Some possible Bible verses to consider hiding are the following: Psalm 4:3b, Psalm 61:8a, Luke 6:27b, Luke 6:31, Psalm 145:18, Romans 12:9, 1 Peter 5:7, Psalm 56:3, Proverbs 17:17, Psalm 136:1, and 1 John 4:10.

Betty B. Robertson
Roanoke, Virginia

Round and Round

Our family loves to sing rounds! Do you remember "Three Blind Mice," "Row, Row, Row Your Boat," and "Frère Jacques?" Rounds are great when there is no piano or other musical instruments in the home. No accompaniment is needed.

What better way to introduce your children to part singing! What better way to make a joyful noise unto the Lord!

Lois Rehder Holmes
Havana, Illinois

Ham It Up

My children delight in performing songs and plays. They all get together and produce their own acts. First we are presented with programs that they designed and decorated, then we are seated to watch the show. Usually one of the family records it with the video camera so the children can watch it later to see how they did. At times it is a pure riot when our three year old literally assumes her role, or when the baby decides to crawl right through the middle of it, hollering. The children like to watch it over and over, many times.

Lisa D. Hughes
Phoenix, Arizona

Well Practiced in the "Arts"

by Norene Morris

As I understand it, "the arts" usually means a platform gathering of talented people who, through hours and hours of concentrated study and practice, finally excel in one or more designated art forms.

Our family took that to heart.

My mother was the accomplished artist. At age twelve, after (believe it or not!) twelve piano lessons from a professor who couldn't play the piano but was an excellent teacher of music at the nearby fledgling California Normal School in California, Pennsylvania, south of Pittsburgh—take a breath—she began playing the piano for Sunday school. At sixteen, she played for silent movies; when at a party, she spent most of her time on the piano bench.

Somehow or other, with a little practice, everyone in our family attributes their talent to Nora George, my talented mother.

Except my husband Paul. He got it from somewhere on his own. No one in his family even played a mouth organ.

In reality, I play piano, as do our two daughters, their dad plays cornet and trumpet (from his days in the school band), and our son plays trumpet and guitar. A musically minded family, or so we thought.

So, when our family had time for fun, did we naturally all gather around the piano? No, we gathered in chairs around the living room.

Everyone picked an instrument of their choice out of the air. Anyone who felt so inspired could opt for the job of conductor of the orchestra. Usually he or she directed with their hands, except the time a ruler happened to be lying on the coffee table and that person seized it and raised this "baton" over the orchestra.

I had always wanted to play the violin so I raised my imaginary violin and tucked it under my chin, bow poised.

Up came Paul's cornet (uh, not the one he played in the band; that one got too close to the Goodwill box and disappeared one day). Paul still had terrific form.

33

Son Allen's drummer hands poised over the coffee table, our daughter Paula lifted her flute, and Sharleen, our oldest, lifted her baton.

I won't guarantee anyone else appreciated our nasal squawks of unrehearsed music but we enjoyed the silliness of it. When we tired of one instrument, we just pulled another from the air. Oh, we were all so versatile!

With such noisy, crazy, wonderful family fun we discovered it really doesn't take much for a family to enjoy being together. The payoff has been wonderful memories to live over and over again of times long past.

Copyright © 1995 by Norene Morris.
Norene Morris, a noted writer of inspirational romance, resides in northeastern Ohio.

The Elevator Lift

Here is a simple activity that is safe, fun, rewarding, and bonding between you and your children. All the needed materials are probably lying around the homestead; before setting up, make sure your children are not watching as the element of surprise is very important.

First, find a board about 2 feet long that is wide and strong enough to support your child. Suspend the board between two stacks of books (not more than 2 inches above the floor) with enough overhang on each end to get a good grip with your hands. Next, blindfold your child and lead him or her into the room to stand on the board while you and your spouse hold each end of the board firmly. Explain that the child is about to go on an elevator ride all the way up to the ceiling and back down again so they need to hold very still. (At this point the child normally wants to hold on to something for dear life so have them place their hands on your head or shoulder.)

Now the fun begins! Slowly lift the board *no more than 1 inch* above the books during the entire elevator ride while you tell them they are getting higher and higher. For an added effect, slowly lower your heads in sync while holding the board. When you feel they've "reached the ceiling," ask the child to touch it. After they reach in midair to no avail, tell them it's time to come down and to please hang on. Slowly raise your heads while explaining that the elevator is coming down and then set the board back on top of the books. Remove the blindfold and have the child tell you all about the ride. If the child gets to watch a sibling or friend take the elevator lift, have them promise not to tell the secret behind this sensational ride.

This is one adventure your children will never forget. I (Nathan) never did, thanks to my parents.

Nathan and Linda Morris
Christiansburg, Ohio

A Tangled Web

The best fun is always uncomplicated, at least that holds true in our house.

Everyone has a supply of ribbon or streamers from a past birthday party and that's all it takes to weave a tangled web. If you don't have at least 25 feet of ribbon, tie what leftovers you have together to achieve that length. On a piece of masking tape on one end of the ribbon write the child's name; on the other end, have the child write a secret message to the detangler.

Draw names to see who will detangle whose ribbon. Then have each child tangle their ribbon all through the living or family room, over and under furniture and toys. When a parent says "Go," the detanglers race against each other to see who can reach the secret message first. (The secret message may promise a special treat or a reward of service.)

Judith Cooper
New York, New York

Knotty Ninjas

Tie a knot in an old sock, scarf, or dish towel and play a knotty game of "ninjas."

Start out with one ninja. On "Go," everyone runs and hides for a few seconds before venturing out to try and find the others. The object is not to get "ninja-ed," in other words, hit with the knotted sock. If you do get hit, you're out while that person picks up your ninja.

Try to get as many ninjas as possible without getting ninja-ed. We always yell "Ninja!" when we jump out and throw the sock. This game, while perfect for snowbound days, also works well outside.

Debra Kopcio
Belvidere, Illinois

Put a Sock In It

As the winter winds howl and play is confined decidedly to the indoors, here's a fun and simple activity: a sock toss! What you will need are socks, of course, stuffing material, and a set of various sizes of bowls and containers.

We usually use old pantyhose to stuff the socks but tissues also work well. Secure the tops of the socks by forming a knot with the sock itself or using garbage bag ties. Make as many stuffed socks as necessary (who doesn't have a dozen mismatched socks?).

Then take the different sized bowls and containers and place some near and some a distance away. Assign the containers numbers from one to 100, depending on the level of difficulty. (Bowls farthest away will have the higher numbers.)

Sock tossers stand behind a designated line and try to land their socks in the containers. The person with the highest score wins, but the containers should be arranged so that all family members have a respectable total. For greater difficulty, graduate to smaller bowls!

Margaret Arman
Grand Rapids, Michigan

Spoon the Balloon?

Living in Michigan we cannot often play outside in the winter. To help run off that extra energy, we play golf or baseball in the house, using balloons and wooden spoons. Another game is to throw a balloon into the air and try to keep it from touching the floor. These started out as games for our boys but we found that adults can get involved, too.

Sue Becker
Britton, Michigan

A Court Potato?

Using wire, fashion a hoop with a hook and hang it from a wall or door. Take turns trying to dunk a balloon or small, spongelike ball.

Under the Bridge

One of our girls' favorite activities with their daddy is called "Under the Bridge." Daddy gets on his hands and knees and makes himself into a bridge as he says, "Can go under...can't go under" or "Can...can't" for short. The girls take turns crawling under his bridge. Suddenly, while saying "Can't" (or whenever he feels like it), he collapses his bridge on top of one of them, amid many, many giggles. Sometimes, instead of a bridge, he will make a giant pair of scissors with his legs. The girls run around him, occasionally getting grabbed by the "horrible scissor lock." Again, there are many giggles.

Bonnie Sherwood
Kenai, Alaska

The New Frontier

One quick boredom buster is to let the kids build a fort in the living or family room. Using blankets, pillows, cushions, and towels, have them use their imaginations to create a supreme fortress...one that can stay up if you're stuck inside for several days.

Adapted from **The Big Book of Family Fun**
by Claudia Arp and Linda Dillow (Thomas Nelson Publishers, 1994). Used with permission by the publisher.

———————

Flashlight Fun

Here's a simple recipe for fun. We all lie on the bed, in the dark, with flashlights turned on!

My young sons love to do this for the longest time making hand shadows. After a long day (or week) at work it's nice because I can just lie there and relax and yet still be close to them.

Mary M. Leech-Roach
Toledo, Oregon

Flashlight Hide-and-Seek

Split up into two groups, usually Mom and Dad against the kids, and each group gets a flashlight. We then turn off all the lights in the house whereupon one group hides while the other counts.

Because the lights are out, the hiding places can be simple, even for little ones; the older children might try to find more elaborate ones. The seekers have to only spot the hiders in the beam of their light for the "catch."

Sometimes, on nice nights, we move the game outside. That's when the camouflage outfits come out—black gloves, black socks over shoes, forest green clothes, and so on. Sometimes the best hiding places are the most obvious, such as someone just leaning against the trunk of a tree. The outside version of this game has become so much fun that we usually get together with our neighbors for a good time.

Lisa Cannon
Inverness, Florida

Rainbow Revelry

The rainbow is such a special symbol in the Bible, and such a wonderful conclusion to the story of Noah, that my children and I decided to see if we could make our own rainbows.

We rustled up all the flashlights in the house and then purchased tissue paper in all the colors of the rainbow at a local craft store. With a little help, the kids wrapped the paper around the beam of the flashlights and held paper in place with rubber bands.

Then, we cut the lights (and turned on our flashlights) and watched the play of the different colors on the wall. By positioning the beams in such a way we created our own rainbows, as well as a wild variety of colors. Only God can create a perfect rainbow, but our feeble efforts were still a lot of fun.

Marie Johnson
Cedar Rapids, Iowa

Night Wrestling

Turn off all the lights throughout the entire house. Have someone shout "Night wrestling!" The game has begun.

Everyone grabs each other and wrestles, tickling and rolling until everyone's sides hurt so much from laughing.

You never know when you'll hear those famous words again, or when the fun will start!

Debra Kopcio
Belvidere, Illinois

Capture the Dessert?

When there seems to be little to do around the house consider having a treasure hunt, with the treasure being a family dessert!

Here's how it works. On several strips of paper, write the clues to the treasure and place them all over the house (and outdoors, too, if the weather cooperates). Children should be told to take turns finding and reading the clues. Note that the first clue is handed to the children. After about six to ten clues, the children should discover a favorite family dessert that will be shared by all. Sometimes the treasure might be all the ingredients needed to make chocolate chip cookies, but whatever the sweet ending, the fun is in the searching!

Be creative with your clues. Consider setting the clues to music, using poetry, acting out a clue, and so on. One example of a clue set to music would be this one, to the tune of "I've Been Working on the Railroad": "I've been working in the house, all the whole day long, I've been working in the house, with the vacuum and a song." The children then find the next clue—Eureka!—by the vacuum.

Steve and Debbie Barnes
Andersonville, Tennessee

Indoor Treasures

Treasure hunts are among our favorite indoor activities. We hide a small treat such as a "fun-size" candy bar, special stickers, or new pencils with designs or sayings printed on them.

Beth Bookout
Santa Rosa, Texas

Animal Hunt

If your children seem to have an unending supply of stuffed animals, this indoor activity is for you.

My family calls this favorite game "Animal Hunt." First, we fill a laundry basket with several stuffed animals. Then one person is in charge of hiding the animals around the room.

When the hiding is complete, the lights are turned out. The "hunters" come into the dark room and use flashlights to find the various animals. As soon as all animals are found, someone else becomes the hider and the game continues.

Sonja Carlson
Monticello, Minnesota

Where Shall We Go Today?

One of the most memorable trips we took as a family was to Hawaii...and we never left home.

Clear out the furniture from your dining room (or similar area) and turn it into a beach by hanging blue fabric over the curtains and on the floor, with brown fabric over that to resemble the beach. (Hint: Sheets work very well.)

Make grass skirts for everyone out of newspaper, leis out of string and Cheerios, and create a palm tree from a lamp by using construction paper. Surfboards can be made from cardboard and are fun toys after you've "returned" from your trip.

Have everyone put on their swimsuits and kids may enjoy wetting down their hair (after riding a big wave). The youngest ones can even wear life jackets! Enjoy lunch at the beach and make the meal especially festive by slicing oranges and placing on the rims of all the drinking glasses.

Next stop for our family: Japan! Let your imagination go and you can go anywhere.

Kim Hempel
Annandale, Minnesota

All Aboard!

Set kitchen, dining room, and folding chairs two by two for as many people playing. One person is the conductor, one is the caboose, and all the rest are passengers. The conductor calls out "All Aboard!" and you're off.

The conductor then proceeds to take pretend tickets (or ones made by children) and the passengers pick their seats. When everyone is seated, the conductor starts the story of where they're going, what they'll see along the way, and what they can do when they get to their destination.

This is great for developing the imagination, not to mention the interesting places you as a family will visit!

Debra Kopcio
Belvidere, Illinois

Summer in Winter

Winters last a long time in New England. But a "beach afternoon" in the bathroom seems to hasten the time until we really are on vacation. Dressed in bathing suits, the children enjoy blowing bubbles and using squirt guns in the bathtub.

Janet M. Bair
Ansonia, Connecticut

Swimming through Winter

Winter can be long in the frozen states. A fun and economical diversion is going swimming as a family. Local health clubs, schools, and even hotels charge a small fee (sometimes no fee—look for coupons in the newspaper) to use their facilities. Take your kids and your goggles and pretend it's summer!

Terry L. Pfleghaar
Elk River, Minnesota

————

Mall Madness

When money is scarce and cabin fever strikes, head for the local shopping mall.

After some window shopping, our family heads for the Cinnabun shop to share a couple of their world-famous, sticky, gooey cinnamon rolls. By the time we finish and get washed up, we have a collective sugar rush and everyone is feeling pretty silly.

Next stop is the picture-taking booth! After cramming inside and jostling for position in front of the camera, we try to come up with the funniest faces possible. Unfortunately, our timing is usually rather bad and when we get the pictures they show us with mouths open and eyes closed as we were telling everyone else what to do.

Thomas, Sally, Andrew, and Jeremy Wilson
Brooks, Oregon

Pet Stop

Many malls have pet stores where puppies are allowed to run free within a confined area. Children of all ages are drawn to animals, and such a stop can relieve the stress of shopping.

Limit the number of pets the children will play with and the amount of time spent with each one. This keeps your family interested in stopping again the next time you go to the mall.

Just wait: Puppies will bring out the child in you, too.

Glenn G. Luscher
Carbondale, Pennsylvania

Stress-free Shopping

Shopping for clothes with my four year old is usually wonderful. But it can be trying when she gets her heart set on something too expensive, or when she chooses an outfit that I think is just awful.

A trip to our local resale shop saves the day. There I never have to tell her that it costs too much, and if she wants to make an occasional fashion faux pas, it's not a big deal.   We get more for our money, help the consigners, help the small business, and recycle. What a great lesson in stewardship!

When my daughter outgrows her clothes, we pass them on to our church clothing bank.

Mila Rowe
Frankfort, Ohio

Rainy Day Resourcefulness

Never-ending is one way to describe those days when you're stuck inside and all the toys and games have suddenly become BORING. Here's one solution.

Fill a chest or trunk with small, inexpensive games and toys. Wrap each one and, as the occasion arises, let each child select one per day. Examples of some inexpensive surprises include coloring books and markers or crayons; liquid bubbles; paper dolls; puzzles; simple craft kits; travel-size games.

Adapted from **The Big Book of Family Fun** *by Claudia Arp and Linda Dillow (Thomas Nelson Publishers, 1994). Used with permission by the publisher.*

Things to Save/Things to Make

Before you're too quick to throw a milk carton away, here's a handy list of other uses for household items. You never know when these items might come in handy for indoor projects or activities.

Save	To Make
Paper towel or tissue rolls	Telescope, megaphone, binoculars, raceways for marbles or ping-pong balls
Oatmeal boxes	Rocket ships, drums
Milk cartons	Pull trains, building blocks, trophies
Shoeboxes	Doll house rooms
Sheets	Tent, sleeping bags, flags and banners
Empty cans, string	Telephone, stilts
Egg cartons	Caterpillar, spider, flowers
Socks, nylons	Sock puppets, old faces, soft balls

Corks, sponges	Boats
Boxes of all sizes	Cage, cars, planes, barn, toss games
Paper clips	Necklaces, other jewelry
Magazines	Artwork projects, cards
Balloons	Indoor volleyball or basketball
Ice pop sticks	Artwork projects, indoor hockey sticks
Eggshells, tiles	Mosaics
Playing cards	Houses of cards

Adapted from **The Big Book of Family Fun** *by Claudia Arp and Linda Dillow (Thomas Nelson Publishers, 1994). Used with permission by the publisher.*

Wall to Wall Art

Every day your child produces several pieces of artwork either at school or home, and you keep many of them. Aside from storing the treasures in an album to be given to the child at a later date, here are some other ways to use that artwork.

In many areas, local print and copy stores offer a calendar-making service; call around and find one near you. Then have your children choose twelve of his or her favorite pieces of artwork and decide which picture should accompany each month. Go together to the copy store and watch your calendar come to life.

The really larger pieces of your child's artwork are ideal for the bigger jobs like wrapping gifts or lining drawers. The ones in the 12-

by 18-inch size range, when covered with adhesive-backed clear vinyl, make great placemats. Standard-sized artwork can serve as separators within a family album or be folded in half and used as note cards.

Smaller pieces of artwork or parts of a larger piece can be used in several different ways. To make a bookmark, cut a piece of artwork to measure about 2 inches by 8 inches, decorate or write a thought on the nonart side, and then cover both sides with clear, adhesive-backed vinyl. Punch a hole in center of top edge and thread yarn or a decorative ribbon though the hole. If the artwork has a Christmas theme, consider making ornaments with it, using this same basic technique.

Make a collage of small drawings, glued to a larger piece of paper, and frame it. Or, if the collage is about 12 by 18 inches, make it into a placemat as explained earlier.

Line glass jars with artwork cut to the circumference and height of the jar, fill jar with potpourri, candies, or other small items, and give as gifts.

Excerpts reprinted with the permission of Family Life *magazine, September/October 1994.*

Personal and Proud of It

Our downstairs playroom, which had off-white walls and curtains, needed some color. After pricing wallpaper and borders, we decided to make our own.

The whole family, including our two-year-old daughter and our one-year-old twin son and daughter, got involved. First we used a feather duster to paint three pale colors all around the bottom half of the room; this gave the walls the effect of wallpaper. Then our older daughter made teal and hot pink handprints on top of the feather dusting and the results were fabulous! Our twins, though, were not to be left out. Using fabric paint that was reasonably priced, our son made teal footprints on the curtains and our daughter made hot pink footprints.

This was a great family activity for us and now we have a precious memory of our children's artwork that is irreplaceable.

Brad and Carleen Peterson
Montevideo, Minnesota

A Group Effort

Stretch a long piece of computer print-out paper on the floor or a large table, gather everyone around, and let each draw and color a part of a collective piece of art, any way they want. The results can be amazing; the shared conversation and fun while doing it is great!

Masterpiece Theater?

Keeping six people interested and entertained is a challenge. We've tried games (too competitive), sports (some of us aren't very athletic), and walks (just plain boring for the older kids). Our favorite activity involves a little creativity and a lot of old-fashioned conversation...and it works for every age level.

First, we clear off the dining room table. Then we get out the colored pencils, dump our collection of plastic stencils in the center of the table, distribute paper, and get busy. Everyone has their opportunity to create a masterpiece! All kids have a great time without competing for Mom or Dad's attention or trying to be the "winner." Even our one year old enjoys listening to the conversation and playing with the plastic stencils.

Cynthia Halliday
Easton, Pennsylvania

A Room with a View

Transform your window into a work of art in just a few easy steps. Decide what you want to see when you "look out" your window...a spring garden, a beautiful landscape, an aquarium filled with tropical fish, whatever is beautiful in God's sight.

Measure the inside surface of your window (and clean it) and then get out your art supplies and cut out and decorate shapes you want in your picture. Working on a surface that is the same size and shape as your window, move shapes around, right sides up, within this area until their arrangement achieves the picture you want in your window. Cut out a piece of clear, adhesive-backed vinyl to the same dimensions as the window, carefully remove its paper backing, and then, adhesive side of the vinyl up, position the shapes, right side down, onto the vinyl, duplicating the same arrangement as on the window-sized work area. When all shapes are in place, carefully pick up the design and adhere it to a clean, dry window.

Adapted from CHILD'S PLAY 6-12 by Leslie Hamilton, Copyright © 1992 by Leslie Hamilton. Reprinted by permission of Crown Publishers, Inc.

A Mosaic of Moses?

Or Noah and his grand getaway, Jonah inside his fishy captor, Solomon and his sumptuous temple? A mosaic is a picture or design made by gluing colored pieces of tile together, or in this case, pasta, buttons, and whatever else you can think of! Favorite Bible stories can come to life for young children when they are the subject of such creative endeavors as mosaics.

Begin by drawing a picture on paper or posterboard and coloring it. If using several types of materials, also decide where each should be placed in the design. Then, dye the materials if necessary. Pour water into small cups, one for each color needed for the design. Add drops of food coloring into the water and stir; add more drops to achieve the desired color. Dip the materials into the appropriate cups and remove them when they have reached the desired color. When dry, use white glue to paste them in the correct area of the design drawn on the paper or posterboard. After the picture is finished, allow it to dry overnight before hanging in an honored place.

Seed Designs

A unique picture can be made using the interesting shapes and colors of seeds and such other dry, hard foods as beans, rice, or pasta.

First, draw a simple design or shape onto paper and decide where each type of seed or food will be placed. When satisfied, glue the design onto a piece of wood or cardboard. Then, working with one element at a time, paint glue onto the design where that element should be and then sprinkle or place the seed or food in place and let dry. When dry, turn over and shake board so loose pieces will fall. If necessary, repeat until the desired amount of that element is in place. Continue to work in this manner until all areas of design are completed.

Apply varnish or polyurethane to completed design. When dry, attach wire or other hanging device to back of design and display on wall.

Egg Carton Extravaganza

Don't throw out those paper egg cartons! A caterpillar, spiders, or flowers can be made from them.

Caterpillar: Cut apart the egg sections and trim edges even; the length of the caterpillar will depend on the number of sections used. Holding one section bottom side up, draw and color the caterpillar's face on front and then poke two holes about 1/2-inch apart on back of head; attach antennae by poking short pieces of pipe cleaner through top of head, bending ends to hold them in place. Hold another section, bottom side up, and draw and color the end of the caterpillar on the back side of the section then poke two holes about 1/2-inch apart on the front side. Use all other sections for the caterpillar's body and, holding them bottom sides up, decorate them accordingly with dots, lines, squiggly shapes, and so on. Poke two holes, 1/2-inch apart, through the front and back side of each body section, making sure front and back holes align with each other. Thread a large-eyed needle with a long length of yarn (any appropriate color); form a large knot in end of yarn. Starting at the caterpillar's head, connect sections by threading yarn through holes on right-hand side of head, body, and end sections, leaving about 1 inch of yarn between sections. Cut and knot yarn end and repeat for left-hand side of caterpillar.

Spiders: Cut sections of carton apart and paint a spider's face on one side of each section. Staying clear of face areas, poke eight holes around top edges of each section, placing holes equidistant from each other and aligning with the holes on the opposite sides of section. Use four black pipe cleaners for each section; thread a pipe cleaner through each set of opposing holes and bend ends to form spiderlike legs. Length of pipe cleaner will depend on size of section and desired length of leg.

Flowers: Cut apart sections of egg carton and cut each into a flower shape. For the stems, poke a hole in center of bottom of each section and thread a green pipe cleaner through each hole; bend end of pipe cleaner to hold in place. Color or paint flowers as desired.

Form open-leaf shapes out of separate pipe cleaners and twist in place onto stems.

A Bouquet of Carnations

One of the easiest (and most fun) flowers to make is the paper tissue carnation. For each flower you will need a tissue (white or colored), a green pipe cleaner, and some yarn to match the color of the tissue.

To make a flower, fold a two-ply tissue in half, lengthwise. Then, working lengthwise from top to bottom, form 1/2-inch accordion-style pleats; secure pleats at center using one end of pipe cleaner. Using your fingernails, gently fray the outer edges of the tissue. Separate the tissue layers and gently pull each up and toward the center of the flower. When all layers are separated, hold base of flower tightly and wrap yarn around it, about 1/2-inch up, thereby holding petals up and in place.

Repeat process until you've made enough carnations for a beautiful bouquet. If desired, use a felt-tipped marker to add color to the fringed edges of the petals.

Preserving Memories

What do you do with a perfect rose presented at a baptism or dedication? A bunch of violets eagerly picked for Mommy by a chubby hand?

Drying flowers or plants is a way to preserve them and the memories they instill. When dry, they can be used for beautiful and unique dried floral arrangements or as decorations for wall hangings, notepaper, and cards. There are three ways to do this: by letting them air-dry, by pressing them, or by drying them using a chemical. Not all methods work for all types of flowers, leaves, or plants; which procedure you use will depend on what you want to preserve and whether you want to maintain its shape or if you want it to be flat. For best results, gather only perfect specimens that have just opened and are not wet.

The easiest drying method for most flowers is to hang them upside down and let them air-dry for a few weeks in a dark, warm, dry place. When done, handle the flowers gently as they are likely to be brittle. Flowers dried with this method can be used to make long-lasting, beautiful floral arrangements. Leaves and grasses are best preserved when left to stand in a solution of one part glycerin and two parts hot water until their color begins to change, a process that can take a few weeks to develop.

Another simple way to preserve flowers and plants is to press them until they are dry. When done, they can be carefully arranged and glued in place to make unique notepaper, cards, or bookmarks; they can even be mounted on a piece of stiff paper which can then be encased in a frame. A very simple method of pressing a flower is to place it between sheets of clean paper (wax paper for delicate specimens) and then insert that between the pages of a thick book or under a stack of several books or bricks until it is dry. If you have many flowers or plants you want to press, consider making a simple plant press. You will need two 16-inch-long by 12-inch-wide pieces of cardboard (for press supports); twenty pieces of cardboard, each the same size as the press supports; thin absorbent paper; and ropes. Alternately layer eight to ten sheets of paper and a piece of cardboard and then place a press support on top and bottom of the entire stack. Carefully position your collected plants, flowers, or leaves between the sheets of paper and then tie everything together tightly, using the ropes. Keep in a warm, dry place, checking every few days until the plants, flowers, and leaves are dry. When done, carefully remove them and keep flat between sheets of paper until you are ready to use.

Adapted from **Hug a Tree** *by Robert Rockwell, Elizabeth Sherwood, and Robert Williams. Copyright © 1986: Gryphon House, Inc., Box 207, Beltsville, MD.*

Presto, Potpourri!

Here's a wonderful use for the strongly scented flowers in your garden. A potpourri is a mixture of dried flowers and other scented items, like spices, herbs, and scented oils, that is placed in an open container for the purpose of scenting the air.

Roses are among the most common flowers to be used in a potpourri, but other suitable flowers include lily of the valley, orange blossom, lilac, carnations, and lavender. Pick the flowers just after they have opened. Remove the petals and then spread them out in a single layer onto sheets of clean absorbent paper or nonmetallic screening. Let then air-dry in a warm, dry room away from drafts or direct sunlight and turn the petals every day or so. When petals are dry, store each type separately in air-tight containers until ready to use.

Many times other dry, scented herbs and leaves (and even woods) are added to the petals; which ones you use will depend on the scent you want to produce. Some popular choices are ginger, bay leaf, pine needles, dried lemon or orange rind, cedar, cinnamon, cloves, and mint. Purchased scented oils can also be used.

Experiment with mixtures of petals, herbs, and other products until the scent they produce is satisfactory. Then put the mixture in an open container or a bag made of lace, net, mesh, or some other open-weave fabric, tying the bag closed so the contents will not spill out.

Why not Make a Family Flag?

Display your family pride for all to see by making a family flag.

To make the flag or banner, cut out a fabric base to size and shape needed, finish its edges with zigzag stitches or a narrow hem, and then decorate it. Use fabric paints to make the design or cut other pieces of fabric in the colors and shapes needed and then glue or sew them in place. Staple the finished flag to a pole and display.

Typically, flags denote seasons or holidays; yours could announce a day special to your family. Work together to think of ways to make your family flag a Christ-centered one: a special flag for Sunday; one that celebrates a baptism or confirmation; a banner depicting a much-loved Bible verse; a flag that celebrates a commitment to Jesus Christ.

No Two Prints Are Alike

This family craft project is not only fun for everyone but a great blessing to the recipients.

Decorate pillowcases, tote bags, aprons, T-shirts, and whatever else you like with the hand- and footprints of the family. Give as gifts to relatives and family friends. You can even decorate plain paper the same way and use as wrapping paper.

All that is needed is fabric paint, plastic (grocery or dry cleaning bags), and the item to be decorated. It's great fun to capture the process on video or still camera. Put the plastic inside the pillowcase or T-shirt so as not to get paint on the opposite side.

Sandi Suganuma
Bellflower, California

A Quilt of Their Own

Before throwing out your family's favorite outfits, cut off some pieces of the fabrics and use them to make a quilt for the person who wore those clothes. When done, every time the person sleeps under the quilt, he or she will dream of the great experiences and events that happened while wearing the clothes.

Beautiful and memorable baby quilts may be made from a beloved grandmother's fabrics. Such quilts then become family heirlooms and are as likely to be displayed on a family wall as a bed.

Built Like a Toothpick!

For kids who think themselves beyond building blocks, here is an activity that will rouse their dormant talents: toothpick architecture!

All that these construction projects require are toothpicks and plasticene or playtime dough to hold joints together. Beforehand, your child may want to sketch ideas for perhaps a castle and its environs, or a future city, perhaps even a location from a Bible story. My kids have created churches, baseball stadiums, "replicas" of famous buildings, and their dream houses.

Use materials from your sewing basket to contruct curtains, carpets, and so on. Doors can be made from baseball cards or similar-sized cardboard.

Elizabeth Kogelmann
Carefree, Arizona

A House of Cards

Have you ever wanted to design your own precarious Tower of Babel, a palace to rival Nebuchadnezzar's, perhaps a customized house of cards? To create these impossible looking structures all you need is cards and a pair of scissors.

Dig up that former deck of fifty-two that now has, say, fifty, and on each long edge of a card make two short clips. Make sure that these short clips are placed at least one inch from the short edges of the card. In the middle of the short edges make a similar short clip. The most important thing is that all the clips on the opposing edges line up with each other. The more cards you prepare, the taller or more elaborate your buildings can be.

Greetings!

Another day inside, another year of greeting cards completed! Say again?

That's right. Make a list of those occasions for which you send cards—birthdays, anniversaries, Valentine's Day, Easter, Christmas, friendship—along with a list of the lucky recipients. Divide the list among you and you're ready to start.

Clear off a table and gather old magazines, old greeting cards, family photographs, plenty of paper in different colors, scissors, glue, a large supply of crayons, pencils, and markers, and your Bible(s) and then design your own cards. Be as creative as possible and generous with your favorite Bible verses.

Adapted from The Big Book of Family Fun *by Claudia Arp and Linda Dillow (Thomas Nelson Publishers, 1994). Used with permission by the publisher.*

Collectibles

Grandparents, relatives, and friends alike always comment on how beautiful and special the cards made by our children are. Over the years we have saved many of these masterpieces and now, when we have a special day and receive a handmade card from them, the memories come flooding back.

Nancy Morast
Kalispell, Montana

Tiny Thank-Yous

Even though our two year old and one year old cannot write, they can still send thank-you notes when they receive a gift.

I help them make a handprint on plain white stationery using bright colors of fingerpaint. When the paint dries, I write a thank-you note from them with a black felt-tipped pen over their handprints. These notes have become wonderful keepsakes for the children's grandparents, and at the same time teaches the children the importance of being thoughtful.

Tina L. Jones
Lebanon, Kentucky

Custom-made Greetings

Many times ready-made cards and notes do not convey the exact feeling or message you want to send. Remedy this by making your own. Start with a suitable paper (from construction paper to a good quality writing paper) in the color of your choice and fold it in half in a cardlike fashion. Pick a size of paper so that, when folded, it will fit a standard size of envelope. Consider scalloping the free edges or cutting the card out in a definite shape, such as a heart, to fit the occasion. Then have fun decorating the card and writing the message you want to convey.

Draw, trace, or cut out and glue pictures to the card; use crayons, colored pencils, or paints; add glitter, lace, dried flowers or leaves, or pieces of fabric or wrapping paper to make the design you want.

Two other decorative techniques are stenciling and sponge printing. To stencil a design, proceed as follows. First, make a stencil. Take glossy paper, fold it in half, and then cut out half the desired shape of the stencil's design from the folded edge out toward, but not beyond, the other edges. Open up folded paper to reveal the entire shape of the stencil's design; experiment with cutouts until you find the one you like. Position the stencil onto the card where you want it to be; hold or tape in place. Using poster paints, lightly dip the end of a small sponge into the paint and then dab the paint over the cut-out area. When done, carefully lift the stencil and let the paint on card dry.

To do a sponge print, you will need an object, such as a leaf, feather, or other thin flat thing that has an interesting shape. Hold the object being printed in place and, using the end of a sponge that has been dipped in poster paint, dab the paint all around the edges of the object. When the object is lifted, its shape will appear on the paper, its outline defined by the placement of the paint. Let paint dry before proceeding with the rest of the card.

Another decorative printing method is to apply poster paint to one side of a flat object that has an interesting shape and texture, lay it paint side down onto a piece of paper, gently press into place, and then carefully remove. What is left on the paper is a lacy version of the object. Let paint dry before continuing.

Veggie-Print Paper

When cut in half either way, some vegetables, such as a pepper, mushroom, or brussels sprout, produce an interesting design. When cut at right angles to its core, an apple produces a starlike pattern and, sliced lengthwise, a broccoli floret resembles a tree or bush. Cut a potato in half and you can carve a wide range of designs into its surface. All of these shapes can be used to make interesting wrapping paper.

Select and cut the desired fruits and vegetables, stretch out a length of craft paper or plain gift wrap, and, using various colors of inked stamp pads or poster paints poured into saucers, stamp the various shapes onto the paper. Adult participation or supervision is required for the cutting of the fruits and vegetables.

Adapted from **The Encyclopedia of Grandparenting** *by Rosemary Dalton and Peter Dalton, Copyright ©* *1992. Used by permission of Bristol Publishing Enter-* *prises, Inc.*

Rainy Day Recipes: Puffy Paint and Homemade Clay

Kitchen projects are favorites in our home. We sometimes make cookies, a cake or pie, whatever we decide that day or week. The children enjoy being part of the decision, the making of the item, and yes, the clean-up afterward. Here are two recipes for fun (and crafts):

Puffy Paint

Mix together equal parts flour, salt, and water. Add to that mixture white glue and food coloring.

Homemade Clay

1 cup flour
1 cup water
1/2 cup salt
1 teaspoon vegetable oil
1 teaspoon cream of tartar
Food coloring

Mix all the ingredients in a small saucepan over low heat. Gently stir until mixture forms a ball. Cool. Remove from pan and knead until pliable. Store in an airtight container (ball will harden if left out).

Bonnie Wentz
Woodbury, Pennsylvania

Cookie Cutter Mobile

First make a clay from cornstarch. Combine 1/2 cup cornstarch, 1 cup baking soda, and 3/4 cup plus 2 tablespoons of water in a pot and stir constantly over medium-high heat. As mixture comes to a boil, it will foam and thicken. Remove from heat when mixture is the consistency of mashed potatoes and pulls away from the bottom of the pot. Allow to cool, then knead clay until smooth on a hard surface dusted with cornstarch. Add more cornstarch if dough is too sticky. Makes 1 1/2 cups of clay; recipe can be doubled. Color clay by adding food coloring either while cooking or kneading. To store, place in plastic bag and refrigerate.

Roll out the clay until it is about 1/8-inch thick; cut out desired shapes, using cookie cutters. Poke hole in top of each shape, using a straw. Transfer shapes to paper towels and let dry until hard. Paint shapes if desired; let dry. Thread yarn through holes at tops of figures and tie ends together. Hang shapes on a branch or clothes hanger, positioning them to balance for a mobile. Shapes can also be used individually as Christmas tree ornaments.

Hands *on* the Walls?

Although our older children brought home from school their plaster of paris handprints as gifts for Mother's Day or Christmas, by the time our younger two were in school the craft had become obsolete. We decided to try it at home, and now we have four delightful sets of handprints that hang proudly in our kitchen. But be warned: This project can sure make a mess!

First, grease the inside of a disposable aluminum pie plate and mix enough plaster of paris (follow package directions) to fill the plate half-full. (Throw out any excess mixture; do not pour it down a drain as it can clog pipes.) Then have your child center his or her hands, fingers spread apart, into the mixture and then carefully lift them out, leaving a good impression of the hands. Using a dowel, poke a hole in the wet mixture above the center of the handprint and about 1 inch in from the top edge. Using a knitting needle, carefully write the child's name and the date below the handprint.

When plaster is dry, lift plaque out of the pie plate, clean off the grease, and paint or decorate it as desired. Thread a length of leather lacing into the hole at the top of the plaque, tie its ends together, and hang the plaque from a hook on the wall.

Elizabeth Kogelmann
Carefree, Arizona

Say Cheese

I enjoy photography as a hobby and, with five children, I am never short on models to pose for me. In fact, the children enjoy creating new settings, moods, and themes for the pictures. Besides costing less than studio portraits, I find that the familiar backgrounds of home (and, of course, the family pets) lend a personal flavor to my pictures. We send these pictures to family and friends in our letters and Christmas cards.

Lisa D. Hughes
Phoenix, Arizona

Portrait of the Artist

Instead of sending family photos inside letters and Christmas cards, we send samples of the children's artwork. Lately we decided to have the kids create self-portraits; the results were so delightful that we had good-quality reproductions made to send to all friends and relatives.

To create the self-portraits, have your budding artists stand in front of a mirror and sketch or use a recent photo and re-create. Encourage them to add some original touches as well, but don't be surprised if a premature mustache or false eyelashes appear.

Linda Doran
Toronto, Canada

A Family Book

Many times a baby book is kept so you won't forget the achievements and milestones of a child. Nothing comparable, though, is kept for the family unit. Establishing and maintaining a *family book* is just as easy to do and can be an invaluable aid in remembering your life together. In fact, such a volume(s) could take the place of separate baby books for each child.

Start with a large book such as a photo album, decorate it as much as you want, and label with your family name and the starting and ending dates of the material contained in the book. Whenever anything significant happens to any member of the family—your first anniversary, the birth of your child, her first words, your new job or the promotion you were hoping to get, kindergarten graduation, that special vacation, and so on—record it in the book with the date of the event as well as a picture or souvenir, some written thoughts of the feelings at the time, or anything else you feel you'd like to preserve. Make the entries as frequent as you want, perhaps even writing a short entry each day. Be sure that every family member feels free to record what he or she thinks is important. When one book is full, start another. You'll have a library of great books that you'll refer to often to read and remember.

From Grandparents, with Love

Here is an indoor activity that is initiated by a grandparent and carried on by the grandchild and other relatives who wish to participate.

Grandparents begin by buying an inexpensive scrapbook for the child, inserting such items as interesting pictures, photos (new and old), articles from magazines, postcards, and greeting cards, and leaving plenty of blank pages for the grandchild or for others to fill in.

The child personalizes the book by writing a journal inside, making colorful headings, dating each entry, and so on. On a regular basis, grandparents and other relatives send the child new pictures that may depict their life or what they enjoyed doing at the child's age.

The child will never forget his or her grandparents—especially if they live far away—with this precious keepsake.

An adjunct to this activity is to let your child browse through old photo albums or scrapbooks. Help him or her name all the faces and tell why those people are in there. At least once a year suggest this activity so your family history becomes well known to the child.

Adapted from **The Big Book of Family Fun** *by Claudia Arp and Linda Dillow (Thomas Nelson Publishers, 1994). Used with permission by the publisher.*

Crafty

by Patsy J. Clairmont

I do crafts. No, wait, that's not quite right. I own crafts. Yes, that helps to bring into focus the blur of materials stuffed into assorted baskets, drawers, and boxes in my attic and basement.

My craft addiction has left partially done projects pleading for completion. I have snarls of thread once meant to be used in needle-point and gnarly looking yarn intended for an afghan. I have how-to books worn from my reading and rereading of the instructions. (I love reading; it's the doing that bogs me down.) Swatches of material, florist wire, paint brushes, grapevines, and (every crafter's best friend) a glue gun—along with a myriad of additional stuff—greet me whenever I open my closet.

Every time I'm enticed into purchasing a new project, I think, *This one I'll do for sure.* I've attempted everything from oil painting, floral arranging, quilting, and *scherenschnitte* (the German art of paper cutting) to quilling.

"Quilling?" you ask. For those of you unfamiliar with it, this craft requires you to wind itsy-bitsy, teeny-weeny strips of paper around the tip of a needle. Once they're wound, you glue the end, using a toothpick as an applicator so your paper coil doesn't spring loose.

Then, with a pair of tweezers, you set your coil onto a pattern attached to a foam board and secure it with a straight pin. You are then ready to start the paper-twirling process over again. To be a good quiller, it helps if you, the crafter, are wound loosely. I believe quillers (at least this one) have to be a few twirls short of a full coil to attempt this tedious art.

You may be wondering how many of those paper tidbits one needs to finish a piece. That depends on the size of your pattern. I chose a delicate, little snowflake. Taking into consideration that I'm a beginner (which is still true of every craft I've ever tried), I decided to select a small pattern and not overwhelm myself. (This would be like saying, "I think I'll go over Niagara Falls in a barrel rather than a tub in hopes I won't get so wet.")

When I started my snowflake, I thought, *I'm going to make one of these for each of my friends and put them on the outside of their Christmas packages.* After five hours and a minuscule amount of noticeable progress, I reconsidered. *I will give these only to my best friends and include them in their gift boxes.*

A week later, I realized I didn't have a friend worth this kind of effort; only select family members would get these gems. And they would be all they'd get. I thought I would also include a contract for them to sign, agreeing to display their snowflakes well lit, under glass, in a heavy traffic area of their homes, all year.

Fifteen hours into my little winter-wonder project, I decided this would be the first and last paper wad I'd ever make...and I'd keep it for myself. It could be handed down in my family, generation after generation, in a time capsule, after my passing. I often wondered who the flake really was in this venture.

I suppose you're asking yourself, *Did she finish it?* Not yet, but I plan to (great inscription for tombstones).

I once attended a retreat where I was persuaded to join a wooden angel craft class. The angel done by the instructor (art major) as an example was adorable. Mine (craft minor) looked like an angel that might join a motorcycle gang.

Even that angel didn't get completed, because they ran out of heavenly parts. She had only one wing and was minus her halo. Actually, it was kind of sad. Today my fallen angel lies at the bottom of a box in my basement, covered with rotting quilt pieces and plastic ivy, still waiting for her ordination. May she rest in peace.

I took a painting class for credit and received an A. Finally, something I could succeed in! Of course, if that were true, why didn't I have a picture to hang?

It hit me that I didn't have a painting anyone could identify, much less display. For one of our projects, we painted apples in a bowl. When I took it home, my friend thought it was a peacock.

I approached the instructor and asked how I had earned an A in her class. "For showing up every week," she responded. She must have the gift of mercy.

Les and I started hooking a two-foot-by-three-foot rug twenty-five years ago. We're almost to the halfway point. We figure, in a joint effort, that we have hooked less than an inch a year and should complete it in the year 2012. You may want to get on our gift list.

I seem to be more into ownership than completion...and then I feel guilty. I've noticed I'm not alone in that. Some kindred spirits could stuff a landfill with their forsaken artistry. I wonder if that's why we have so many garage sales and so much garbage in this country. We sell off and throw away our unfinished business, and then we go buy more.

Words like *responsibility, follow through,* and *moderation* get lost in the shuffle as I push back one box of crafts to move in my newest project. Every time I haul out or hide away another abandoned endeavor, it reinforces a negative quality within me.

Besides, what happened to the notion "Waste not, want not?"

That's a great line. I wonder how it would look in cross-stitch? Oops, there I go again.

―――――――

A Different Type of Fun?

Dust off that old manual or electric typewriter and a day inside becomes like no other!

If your child knows the alphabet, they will have a blast typing their name and all sorts of crazy words. They can type notes to siblings, relatives, and to you. If they're receiving spelling homework, they can type their list of words for the week. With a little supervision, they can also use the home computer.

Adapted from **The Big Book of Family Fun** *by Claudia Arp and Linda Dillow (Thomas Nelson Publishers, 1994). Used with permission by the publisher.*

Shower Script

My two year old hated to take baths until he received a gift of a package of spongelike numbers and letters. When wet, these numbers and letters stick to the shower walls.

Now he can hardly wait to get in the tub with his floating (and sticking) alphabet. As time went on, my sixteen and thirteen year olds got involved and now we have a shower message board. I've seen the sponge forms arranged in numerical and alphabetical order; I've found the message "I love you." (Even Dad does it now.)

What will be the next mystery message? Whatever it is, we've created a family memory.

Linda Peterson
Minatare, Nebraska

The Letter Stops There

If your child is into writing stories, maybe she or he has something to say to the President...of the United States. Not only is this an activity that is a privilege of being a member of a democracy, but your child will be thrilled when he or she gets a letter back from the White House!

Our children have written as part of a class at school, but there's no reason why families can't also put pen in hand. Remember, the Bible encourages us to pray for our leaders, but all of us—no matter how small—should let them know just how we feel. Here's the address:

> The White House
> 1600 Pennsylvania Avenue
> Washington, D.C. 20500

Margaret Arman
Grand Rapids, Michigan

Three Shorts, Three Longs, Three Shorts! (In other words, "HELP!")

The Morse code has been used for well over a century and now your home can reverberate with messages à la Morse.

Don't be dismayed; the code is easy and kids learn fast! The dots, of course, are short flashes or sounds; the dashes are longer ones.

The Morse Code

A .-	C -.-.	E .	G --.
B -...	D -..	F ..-.	H ....

I ..	P .--.	W .--	4 ....-
J .---	Q --.-	X -..-	5 .....
K -.-	R .-.	Y -.--	6 -....
L .-..	S ...	Z --..	7 --...
M --	T -	1 .----	8 ---..
N -.	U ..-	2 ..---	9 ----.
O ---	V ...-	3 ...--	0 -----

Name that Day

In order to change the daily routine into an extraordinary experience or to improve the overall attitude and atmosphere of your home, "Name that Day!"

Each day of the week, Sunday through Monday, takes on a new meaning when, within your own family circle, you have "named" each day. Here are some examples:

Monday—Marvelous Monday
Tuesday—Terrific Tuesday
Wednesday—Wonderful Wednesday
Thursday—Thoroughly Thankful Thursday
Friday—Fabulous Friday
Saturday—Sweet Sleep-in Saturday
Sunday—Sacred Sunday

Enjoy seeing the reaction on your children's faces as you say, for example, "Good morning, today is Terrific Tuesday!"

Kathryn Bechtel
Muncy Valley, Pennsylvania

It's Dinnertime!

Children want to help and dinnertime is an ideal time for them to practice their skills for, no matter what the age, there is an age-appropriate job either before, during, or after dinner. The younger ones can set the plates and silverware and help with other decorative chores such as centerpieces and napkin folding; the older ones can also help with the food preparation and serving. All can take turns clearing and cleaning the dishes. And during this time, you are all together sharing conversations and being a family. Do not be too critical of a job being done by one less experienced than you; this is how they learn the job and you learn to be more patient.

One particularly fun activity is folding napkins decoratively. Here are two ways to fold a napkin.

Napkin roll: Take a square, stiff napkin and, starting at one corner, roll it toward the opposite corner. Fold rolled napkin in half and insert it into a glass.

Fan: Fold a stiff, square napkin in half. With folded edge to your right and open edge to your left, accordion-pleat the napkin from top to bottom. Grasp pleated napkin at right-hand folded edge and twist it. Fan will automatically open and spread apart. Insert twisted end in a napkin ring.

For a centerpiece, rely on your imagination and items already in your home. Use fresh or artificial flowers or greens; arrange fruits or vegetables in a dish or platter; cluster various stuffed toys or special figurines or statues. Make sure the centerpiece is low enough or has enough see-through spaces for people on all sides of the table to see each other.

Adapted from The Encyclopedia of Grandparenting *by Rosemary Dalton and Peter Dalton, Copyright © 1992. Used by permission of Bristol Publishing Enterprises, Inc.*

Break the Rules Night

Dinnertime with the family all sitting down together is an important time for many families. But sometimes this time can seem like a constant battle to reinforce our children's table manners. To make dinnertime more fun, we have a once-a-month "Break the Rules Night."

Instead of being told not to sing at the table, we sing instead of talk, or hum, or whistle. If someone feels like getting out of their chair to do a little dance for a minute, that's okay, too. Instead of being told to hold the fork properly, it's eat with your fingers night!

The abundance of giggling makes up for any mess!

Nancy Van Cott
New Milford, Pennsylvania

Under an Assumed Name

To diffuse tension and discourage bad behavior at the dinner table we play a game we call "Assumed Names." Each family member chooses an alias and must be referred to in conversation by that name throughout the meal. Anyone using a family member's real name is out but can still continue enjoying the fun of hearing others get caught in the same way.

Brenda Picazo
Springville, New York

Pick a Pair of Pears

Because of home schooling my boys I invented this idea for studying

73

homonyms. On a large piece of construction paper I painted a green tree without leaves and then glued pieces of bark to the tree's trunk. I taped this to the window by our dinner table and entitled it "Pair Tree, Pick a Pair of Pears." When someone would come up with a new set of homonyms, I would print them on a small yellow, construction-paper pear and then glue the pear to the "Pair Tree."

It soon became a family game that had all of us excited; all of us would look for new pairs while reading books, newspapers, or magazines. Even the grandparents, after seeing the tree, would call on the phone with another set of pairs.

Lori Haynes
Pine Mt. Club, California

The Sillier, the Better!

Have a picnic in the family room. Invite special dolls or stuffed animals to join in the fun. For entertainment, turn on snappy music and dance.

While your VIP guests are there, consider having an Easter egg hunt when it's not Easter. Hunt for anything that comes to mind.

Have the children and their guests form a circle on the floor and have each tell you a story. Write down their words and read it back to them, and then mail it to a relative or loved one.

Linda J. Beck
Chicora, Pennsylvania

Homework Is Fun?

One solution to the ever-present homework dilemma—"It's due TO-DAY??"—is to create a homework center at the hub of activity, usually the family kitchen.

It's simple: Most kids don't want to be relegated to their rooms to study when the rest of the family is congregating somewhere else.

A homework center could be created right on the kitchen table. Take a file box and fill with school supplies; this box can be easily removed when homework is finished. While Mom or Dad is cooking dinner, she or he can be available to answer questions that may arise and can also offer encouraging words.

Adapted from **The Big Book of Family Fun** *by Claudia Arp and Linda Dillow (Thomas Nelson Publishers, 1994). Used with permission by the publisher.*

Fun Food

Make any meal more fun by decorating the food or make it look different. Breakfast and luncheon foods are particularly easy to work with. Here are several suggestions.

*Use cookie cutters to cut shapes out of bread (toast them if desired) and use them to make sandwiches.

*Spread cream cheese on bread or toast and decorate with faces made from pieces of dried fruit, nuts, or pieces of cereal.

*Make a volcano from a bowl of cereal by mounding the cereal around the edges of the bowl, making a depression in the middle, then filling the hole with milk.

*Wrap a pancake around a cooked sausage and then serve with your favorite syrup.

*Use waffles to make sandwiches with foods like eggs, jelly, peanut butter, or breakfast meats as the filling.

*Cut fruits into pieces and serve on wooden skewers; skewer cut pieces of luncheon meats, pickles, vegetables, and cheeses.

*Spread cream cheese and olives on a soft tortilla and roll up.

*Stuff celery with peanut butter or cream cheese and spread raisins or other dried fuits over the filling.

Words of Wisdom Cookies

Make your family literally eat their words! Allow about two hours to complete (this might be a perfect project for Family Fun Night). Start by having everyone write a short prayer, wish, or other inspirational message on 2-inch by 1/2-inch pieces of freezer wrap.

To make the cookies you will need:

    3 egg whites
    3/4 cup sugar
    1/8 tsp salt
    1/2 cup butter or margarine, melted
    1/4 tsp vanilla
    1 cup sifted flour
    1 Tb instant tea
    2 Tb water

In a medium bowl, combine egg whites, sugar, and salt. Stir in, one at a time, the butter, vanilla, flour, tea, and water. Chill for at least 20 minutes. On a greased baking sheet, drop a slightly rounded teaspoon of dough for each cookie, keeping them about 4 inches apart. Using the back of a spoon, spread the dough for each cookie very thin until it is is about 3 inches in diameter. Bake 5 minutes at 350°F or until edges turn light brown.

Remove immediately to a wire rack; cookies should be paperthin. Quickly place one of the messages on paper in the center of the cookie. Fold cookie in half to form a half-moon. Grasp the rounded edges of the moon between the thumb and forefinger of one hand.

Place the forefinger of the other hand at the center of the folded edge. Push in, making sure the cookie puffs out. Keep the forefinger in place while bringing the edges of the fold downward around the forefinger. Place each cookie in a section of a muffin tin. Open edges up until the cookie cools completely.

Adapted from **The Encyclopedia of Grandparenting** *by* **Rosemary Dalton and Peter Dalton, Copyright © 1992. Used by permission of Bristol Publishing Enterprises, Inc.**

Job Jar

To avoid arguments when it comes to housecleaning chores, develop a Job Jar. Have a family meeting to discuss what the household chores are and how necessary it is for everyone to pitch in and help. Write each job to be done on a separate piece of paper and put it in a jar or another appropriate container. Each day (or on particular days) have each family member select a job from the jar. Before putting it back, indicate who did the job and the date. This way you can rotate the jobs so that each gets a turn.

Therese Cerbie
Harrington Park, New Jersey

The Family that Cleans Together...

Spend time together as a family and clean the house, too! To make the task easier, go together from room to room (and go by twos) and divide the chores in each room. While you're toiling, play your favorite Bible stories or Christian music on tape or sing songs.

Sandy Umber
Springdale, Arkansas

Reverse Roles

One way to make children and parents appreciate each other is to reverse roles for one day. The children become the parents and the parents become the children.

During this time the new "parents" tell the new "children" what to wear, what to eat, what jobs to do, when to go to bed, and so on. In turn, the new "children" act as normal children tend to do: They find other things to do, ask questions, take their time, and complain.

At the end of the day each will be more appreciative of the other and their responsibilities and their frustrations.

The Book of Family Fun

outdoors

**God has provided us with a world of beauty. . .
and the tools to discover its many wonders.**

Turn Off the TV and Turn On to Life!

A few years back our family felt a strong conviction to turn the TV off permanently. You know what? We never run out of things to do.

The Lord has blessed us with a fourteen-acre farm on which we raise sheep, pigs, chickens and roosters, rabbits, ducks, cats, dogs, guineas, peacocks, a parakeet, goats, and three wonderful children. There are many chores to be done, but more times than not, these chores turn to fun.

As the days heat up, we walk hand in hand through the woods admiring God's handiwork. We find just the right spot to open our picnic basket and stop to eat while we watch the squirrels scurry around and the beavers build their dam. Next thing you know, the kids are swimming in the creek, Dad's fishing upstream, and Mom's walking barefoot in the cool, clear water.

It's not long until it's time to start cutting wood to get ready for winter. We turn this chore into an assembly-line operation so we can get finished fast (and then play). There are trees to be climbed, vines to be swung on, and flowers to be picked. Since the garden by this time has nothing left in it except overripe, soft vegetables, we take advantage of what is left: We have the messiest, stinkiest food fight you've ever seen! Although no one likes raking too much, everyone loves jumping in the big piles of colorful leaves.

As the nights get cooler, we build a big fire and roast wieners and marshmallows, and pretend not to notice when the dogs swipe one or two. We eat, laugh, and sing at the top of our lungs to our Lord who has granted us the day. When the snow falls, we grab the sleds to race each other down to the bottom of the hill. Dad gathers up a big bowl of snow for me and I add a little sugar, milk, and a dash of vanilla extract. The result is God's homemade ice cream!

On rainy days we move the furniture out of the way for a silly "dance-a-thon" or we make different crafts. The most fun is at night when all the lights are out and the rain is falling and you can see the others only when the lightning flashes. For extra fun we pop a big batch of popcorn on the stove but we leave the lid off! Everyone has to run around catching the flying popcorn in their mouths or dodging the flying kernels.

At our house God is first in all things and family comes next. God has given us our family to enjoy, love, and care for while we wait for Him to come and take us to our *real home*...what a family gathering that will be!

Donna and Jerry May
Greensburg, Kentucky

Hunt and Peck

Here's a great outdoor activity that gets even greater when you use your God-given imagination!

A nature scavenger hunt takes only ten minutes or so to prepare and will last for at least an hour. First, make a list of objects for your children to find in your yard or playground. Give them defined boundaries that are safe for their ages.

For small children who do not yet recognize words, use crayons and draw objects for the hunt. Give each child a backpack or a bag and send them off on a real adventure. The following items are popular with six through eight year olds:

Rocks (different colors)

Something fuzzy

Twig with no leaf

Twig with a leaf

Leaves (specified colors)

Pine cone

Pine needle

Dead weed

Green weed

Dead bug

Moss

For ten year olds and up, you might add these requests:

Lilac leaf

Perennial flower (or annual)

Bark from a maple tree

Deciduous leaf (one example)

Clover

Mint leaf (or other spice leaves)

Adapted from **The Big Book of Family Fun**
by Claudia Arp and Linda Dillow (Thomas Nelson Publishers, 1994). Used with permission by the publisher.

Backyard Scavenger Hunts

Have a scavenger hunt right in your own backyard. Depending on the season and the age of the children taking part, make a list of items to be found. For example, in the spring include things like flowers, baseball or other sporting equipment, and gardening tools; in the winter, list a snow shovel, broken twig, and an icicle. Also decide whether the items need to be collected or just discovered and then checked off the list.

Adapted from **CHILD'S PLAY 6-12** *by Leslie Hamilton, Copyright © 1992 by Leslie Hamilton. Reprinted by permission of Crown Publishers, Inc.*

Letter Day Hunt

Almost any age group and any size family can participate in this activity. A small family can go out as one group or a large family can divide up with Mom or Dad or older sibling taking small groups.

Before you leave for your neighborhood outing, decide what your letter will be and make an appropriate list of things to collect that begin with that letter. If you have more than one group, make copies and send each group out. Each group has to find all the items on the list. Here's an example of a possible list for the letter C:

Cotton ball

Corn flake

Crayon

Card

Candy

Cartoon

Cookie

Come back and celebrate with a snack beginning with your letter...like cookies and cocoa!

Kent and Kathy Slick
Glenpool, Oklahoma

Glad Day

It was a snow day. Dad was home, Mom was home, and the girls were home. The snow looked so inviting but we could not justify buying sleds for six of us for one day of play. Still....

Dad suggested we each dress warmly and grab a large, heavy-duty trash bag. Off to the hills we went! After clearing the debris from our runs, the bigger "kids" sat on top of the bags and prepared for their run. The smaller ones sat inside the bags. No need to wait your turn in the cold for sister to return the sled to the top of the hill!

After we had our fill of fun, we stuffed the bags with the snow-crusted mittens, scarves, and caps and carried them to the washer, without any dripping trail. Glad Mom, glad Dad, glad girls, glad day.

Lynn Sansone
St. Peters, Missouri

Follow the Map

Designate someone to mark or hide things in the snow and draw a map for the rest to follow in finding the clues to the buried treasure. Be sure to make false tracks in the snow to cover the real trail to the treasure. If you're adventuresome, look up copies of real animal prints in nature books and copy those. The treasure could be an old box filled with costume jewelry or small toys and puzzles.

Adapted from CHILD'S PLAY 6-12 *by Leslie Hamilton, Copyright © 1992 by Leslie Hamilton. Reprinted by permission of Crown Publishers, Inc.*

Picnic In the Snow

Every winter our family has a special event that we always antici-pate—our annual snow picnic! Equipped with a sled, a homemade piñata, and a Coleman stove, we drive to our favorite picnic spot in the mountains. There we feast on chili soup and then hot chocolate with marshmallows to keep us warm. After lunch, we go sledding and take turns trying to break the candy- and treat-filled piñata that we have tied to a rope and hung over a tree.

Lori Richard
Mt. Pleasant, Iowa

The Snow Family

After a good snowfall, make snowpeople to represent all the mem-bers of your family, even the cat. Let your imagination roam when choosing objects for eyes and other facial features: rows of red holly berries for lips, pine cones for noses, pine bows for hair, and use old clothing to dress the people. Have them standing, lying down, or even sitting on a bench. When finished, have a neighbor take a picture of your family and their twins.

Back to Basics: Fox and Goose

I remember playing this winter game as a child, but I certainly didn't remember all the rules. My kids, who learned the game at school, were pleased to offer these instructions. All you need is a fresh snowfall and warm winter gear to play.

Make a large circle in the snow with your boots, large enough for kids (and adults) to run around. Inside that circle stomp out several paths so that the circle now resembles a sliced pizza. Now you're ready for action.

One person is the fox and the other the goose, and, of course, the fox will be chasing the goose. However, the fox can only run on the established pathways to tag the goose; the goose must also use these pathways but can also retreat to the center where he or she may not be tagged (a safety zone). Once the goose is tagged by the fox, the fox becomes the goose and the goose becomes...the fox!

Ellen Caughey
Harrington Park, New Jersey

Snow Art

Bring out all your squirt guns, fill them with colored water, and have a ball using them to "draw" pictures in the snow. Draw people, landscapes, your dream car, or anything you want.

Ice Skating Today

Once you know the ground is frozen, choose a level, shaded area that has no rocks and surround it with logs or mounds of packed snow. While weather is still freezing, flood the area with some water and let freeze overnight. Do this several times until the ice is a few inches thick. To keep the rink in good shape, fill holes with water and let freeze. Be sure to take care that your hose doesn't freeze. Beginning skaters should wear bike helmets for protection.

Your Very Own Exercise Course

Now you can turn your own backyard (or a nearby field or playground) into an exercise course tailor-made by and for you and your family.

Start by drawing a map of the area, noting things like trees, basketball hoops, or other landmarks within the area and designate them to be the individual exercise stations along the course. Then decide what type of exercises you want (and need) to do and assign a particular exercise to each landmark; note these on your map. Give a warm-up exercise such as stretching for the first station; the last should be a cool-down, gentle type of exercise. In between, make use of each landmark in an appropriate way. For example, shoot several baskets into the basketball hoop if there is one; run a few circles around a garage; do four cartwheels in an open flat area.

So that you don't have to bring the map with you, make a sign for each station describing each exercise and place it next to the station. When you get bored with your course, change it and the type of exercises.

Adapted from CHILD'S PLAY 6-12 *by Leslie Hamilton, Copyright © 1992 by Leslie Hamilton. Reprinted by permission of Crown Publishers, Inc.*

Sardines

Now the grandmother of seven, I remember having a lot of fun with all ages of children playing "Sardines." It is the opposite of "Hide-and-Seek" and you need a large space in which to play the game.

One person hides while everybody else closes their eyes and counts. After the count everyone spreads out to look for the hidden one and whoever is successful quietly crawls in with him or her. One by one the hunters disappear until only one is left hunting and that one is the hider for the next game.

Kathy Erickson
Unalakleet, Alaska

Do-It-Your-Way Hopscotch

On a sidewalk or driveway, draw a row of connecting shapes alternating from a square to a triangle to a circle. The row can be straight, curved, or zigzagged; the shapes should be about 12 inches across. Determine what activity or action should be done in each type of shape. For example, if you land on a circle, you have to do four knee bends; if you land on a square, you have to hop up and down ten times. This game can be played with one or more people. Players jump from one space to the next along the course. You can play simultaneously, giving each one a one-minute head start or each player can go through the entire course alone and the one who does it fastest, wins.

Adapted from **CHILD'S PLAY 6-12** *by Leslie Hamilton,*
Copyright © 1992 by Leslie Hamilton. Reprinted by
permission of Crown Publishers, Inc.

Circular Volleyball

Use a balloon as the volleyball and have all but one of the players on one side. One by one, have each player hit the balloon to another player and then go around the net to the other side. When all but one player are on the other side, start over again, working toward the first side. See how fast you can get the players from one side to the other and then back again.

Shake and Bake! Take It Downtown!

That's basketball jive, and just the ticket for a nice, not-too-hot day.

One game the whole family can play on an outdoor basketball court is "Around the World." The rules are simple: Place stones at seven positions on the court. Players position themselves at the various stations and attempt to sink baskets from those spots. When they succeed, they move to the next station. The first player to sink baskets from all seven—around the world—wins.

You may want to label the spots for fun-sounding global destinations, or even places where your family would like to take a vacation. For younger players, position some stations within close range of the hoop, or make a separate set of stations for them.

Then, there's the old standby, "H-O-R-S-E." Players stand at various locations on the court and try to make a basket. When he or she succeeds, the other players have to make a basket from that very spot, or they're on their way to spelling "HORSE." Each time you miss (when someone else has made a basket) you receive a dreaded letter.

The first person to spell the word is out of the game, and so it goes until one is left.

Keep in mind you don't have to spell one word. You might try spelling your last name, a nickname, a chore to accomplish around the house (loser or winner gets to do it!), and so on.

Andrew Wilse
Englewood, New Jersey

Simon Speaks!

The game of Simon Says is always fun, and the faster it is played, the better!

A small group of children and adults works well, and one person is chosen to be Simon.

Simon stands facing the line of players and begins by saying, "Simon says (do *something*, such as touch your nose, tickle yourself, jump up and down, raise your right arms, and so on)." Everyone playing must do what Simon says. However, if Simon simply says, "Stand on tiptoe (or another motion)" without saying "Simon says," everyone should remain motionless. Players who fail to do what Simon says after Simon said "Simon says," as well as those who do what Simon says when Simon didn't say "Simon says," are out of the game!

Of course, the faster Simon rattles off commands, the harder it is to remember whether Simon indeed said "Simon says...." Simon should make the actions as crazy and funny as possible!

Green Light Means Go!

Another traditional outdoor game (the rules of which may be long forgotten) is Red Light, Green Light.

To begin, choose a fairly large playing field and position the person who is the "stoplight" at least 25 feet away from the other players who are lined up shoulder to shoulder. The "stoplight" turns his or her back to the other players and shouts "Green light!" At that, the players start to run toward the "stoplight." At any time the "stoplight" may turn around and shout "Red light!" If the "stoplight" sees any player running, that player becomes the "stoplight." The object is to run past the "stoplight" without being caught.

Red Rover, Red Rover

Remember this one? This game is best suited for large groups such as Sunday school classes and youth groups. Red Rover can be played on a beach or grassy field, and only adult supervision is required.

Divide the group into two teams; have each team link arms. Have the teams line up, facing each other, about 25 feet apart. One person on each side is designated the caller, and one caller begins the game by yelling, "Red Rover, Red Rover, send (name of person on opposing team) right over!"

At that, the person summoned makes a dash toward the opposing line of players, looking for a weak link in the human chain. If he or she breaks through the chain, that person brings back to the home team a player from the opposing team. At the end of a designated playing time, the team with the most players wins.

Be Square!

The forgotten game of Four Square is about to be revived in your driveway, alley, or nearby playground. Watch out: It's addictive, and a tournament may be the event of the summer!

To create a "four square," take a piece of chalk and draw a big square. Within that square draw four equal-sized squares. To play the game all you'll need is a medium-sized rubber ball or basketball.

To play, the person in the top right square is the server. He or she serves the ball by letting the ball bounce once in his or her square and then batting it to another square. Play continues until the server or another player hits the ball out of bounds or fails to return a shot. Whoever misses goes automatically to the beginning or lower right-hand square or to the end of the waiting line outside the entire square; everyone then advances to the next square, in a clockwise direction. The object, of course, is to see how long you can remain as server, and to get the server out.

Capture the Flag

This is one of those traditional childhood outdoor games that you may have forgotten. For a large group you can't beat this activity.

Find a large field and divide it in half with some sort of line. (A smaller area is, of course, advised for younger participants.) On each baseline of each side, position one flag per person on that side. Flags may be made by taking old rags and taping them to a stick and then sticking the sticks in the ground. Space flags evenly across each baseline.

The game begins when players attempt to cross the center line and "capture" an opposing player's flag. If the player is tagged by an opposing player before obtaining the flag, that player must stand behind the row of flags on the opposing player's side. The team with the most flags wins!

Let the Games Begin!

The Outrageous Olympics, that is. This is the only "olympiad" with no traditions and no rules...because you make them up as you go. All you need is one eager family with energy and imagination to burn. (This activity also works well at a neighborhood block party.)

Lead off with the youngest child holding a torch fashioned from rolled-up newspaper covered in aluminum foil. After the "opening ceremonies," divide into two teams for the crazy relays. The first person in line should be the one to devise a particular race. You might hop on one foot across the yard, walk backward while flapping your arms, balance a book on your head while singing, carry a ball on a spoon on all fours, you name it.

The necessary ingredients for any activity are have fun, laugh a lot, and give lots of hugs. During the final closing celebrations, be sure that everyone gets an award.

Hip-Hip-Hooray!

When our son joined a football team, two of his younger sisters wanted to be involved in sports, too, so they signed up to be cheerleaders for their brother's team. Not only did this arrangement save us a lot of driving around to different practice and game sites, but the entire family (even Grandpa) enjoyed the evenings out together. We all had a delightful time and cheered them on even when they didn't win. The glow on their faces proved how much this boosted their self-esteem.

Lisa D. Hughes
Phoenix, Arizona

Paper Airplane Mania
(and other crazy contests)

Create airplanes from leftover school notebook paper. Hold a contest to see whose plane stays in flight the longest and flies the farthest.

While you're at it, set up various other events such as the discus throw using paper plates; a "diving" meet with each person tossing jelly beans into a container of water; the "shot put" using a marshmallow; a one-yard dash by pushing a type of breakfast cereal across the ground with the nose; a javelin throw using straws; and finally, a standing high jump using doughnuts suspended from a rope line, about 4 inches above the mouth (one bite wins, using no hands).

Betty B. Robertson
Roanoke, Virginia

Surf's Up

One much-anticipated event of our summer is a family trip to a beach. Since "our beach" is on the ocean, body surfing has become a favorite activity for all of us.

To catch a wave, go out just beyond the place where the waves begin to break. The first attempts should be made in an area with a sandy bottom and waves around 3 feet high.

With your body facing the shore, keep your eyes on the waves coming toward you. When the one you want gets close, lean forward, push off from the bottom, and swim several quick strokes to get your body moving at the same speed as the wave. The wave will not pass beneath you, but will carry you effortlessly forward! Drop your head, hunch your shoulders down into the water so they are lower than the rest of your body, and extend your arms straight ahead. Once you're moving along with the forward slope of the wave, lift your head up and enjoy the ride.

Susan Kutkowski
Plainview, New York

Slippery Fun

Guess what? Your own backyard could be the future site of one of the world's best waterslides! Just dig out that old plastic shower curtain and the fun is about to begin.

Position the plastic "slide" over an area of the yard that boasts an incline, preferably. Wash the plastic down with a hose, or, better yet, position a sprinkler nearby so slide is always wet.

Have kids and adults line up and slide down first on seats to test slipperiness. The fun begins when one person is leader and everyone has to follow motions down the slide.

The dog days of summer have never been cooler!

Bubble Battle

Our family has the best times with a bubble battle. First I make up a huge batch of soap solution using a ratio of one part dish soap to ten parts of water, with a teaspoon or two of glycerine for better bubbles. Then we go out in the backyard with a timer, empty straw baskets, and some slotted spoons and spatulas. With the timer set for 5 minutes, the attacking team makes bubbles with the baskets and spoons while the defending team chases the bubbles and demolishes them with the spatulas. When the timer rings, the teams change roles.

Sara Everett
Hesperia, California

Jumping High!

by Veda Boyd Jones

Jumping on a trampoline is the next best thing to flying. The world is viewed from an entirely different angle.

Backyard trampolines are fun for the entire family. They can also teach skills and coordination that transfer to other sports. Jumping on a trampoline develops similar techniques used in diving, gymnastics, and pole vaulting. Body control and timing can transfer to basketball and soccer. Skiers, football players, and runners can benefit by gaining stamina and leg strength. Eye coordination can help with tennis and baseball. Bouncing is also a good aerobic activity. But before you kick off your shoes and climb up on the trampoline bed, you should know the safety rules.

The number one rule is that only one person should jump on the trampoline at a time. The bed of the trampoline has to give with the jumper. If two are jumping, the bed may be on the rebound from the first person and bounce the second person before he's ready and that can be dangerous.

Whether the trampoline is round, square, or rectangular, the number two rule still holds: Jump in the middle and keep your eyes on the edge of the trampoline in front of you. Don't look down at your feet or you may lose your balance.

The third rule is never to jump off the trampoline to the ground. After jumping, your body is used to the extra throw that the trampoline gives you. There's no give in the ground. Your body can't absorb the shock of the hard surface. Climb on and off the trampoline.

How do you bounce? Easy. Start in the center and jump up. Bring your arms up and forward then circle outward to maintain balance and give you height. It's the same principle as pumping to get going in a swing. When you come down on the trampoline keep your feet a shoulder's width apart. When you go up again, and you'll be higher this time, bring your feet together and point your toes. These are known as standing bounces and you should keep your bounces low until you learn control.

There are several fundamental body positions. Practice the position on the trampoline bed before you jump and you will know how it is supposed to feel when you land. Here are a few of the fundamental bounces.

Seat drop: From a low bounce, land in a sitting position with your legs straight ahead of you, your hands on the bed beside you, and lean forward slightly. On your next bounce, stand up.

Knee drop: Assume a kneeling position when you land. Keep your back straight. Again, on your next bounce, stand up.

Pirouette: When you are doing a standing bounce, try this. At the height of your bounce, turn your body halfway around. Don't travel, but stay in the center of the trampoline.

Tuck position: At the height of your standing bounce, bring your knees up and hold them, much like you'd do for a cannonball into a swimming pool. As you go down, lower your feet so you can land standing up.

Straddle pike position: At the height of your bounce, bring your legs up as if you were sitting on air. Point your toes and spread your legs as far apart as you can. Touch your toes, then land in the standing position.

There are many positions for you to try, but before you ever try advanced positions you must master the easier ones. Never try flips or somersaults without instruction from a qualified teacher.

Bouncing on a backyard trampoline is fun and good exercise for the entire family. Follow the safety rules and enjoy!

Veda Boyd Jones of Joplin, Missouri, is a popular author of inspirational romance.

"I'm Bored!"

Why not suggest ways your child can make money...by being outdoors? Here are some ideas, but be sure to have your own brainstorming session as well:

Have a yard sale

Grow vegetables and sell to friends and neighbors

Do yard work (mow, pull weeds, plant flowers)

Water yards and plants on regular basis for neighbors

Teach younger children a sport (soccer, tennis, basketball)

Provide the entertainment for birthday parties

Walk the dog

Adapted from **The Big Book of Family Fun** *by Claudia Arp and Linda Dillow (Thomas Nelson Publishers, 1994). Used with permission by the publisher.*

History Comes Alive

In the fall we drew the ship, the *Mayflower*, to scale on the street in front of our house. We drew the decks and the hold of the ship as best as we could from the drawings we found in the library to use as references. We and the children lay down side by side to see how the settlers would have slept in the real ship. We measured the small space (about the size of a single bed) that each adult would have had and then to have a meal as a family in that space. We cooked on our grill (a brazier) and had "hardtack" biscuits with our meal.

For vacations we camp in a wooded area and we have found that reading aloud together as a family around the campfire is a very special activity that binds us together. Most recently we read the "Little House" books because they lend themselves well to the wooded area. We were able to make Indian costumes and act out the chapters about the Indian territory.

It is fun to re-create history and do things the way they did way back then. It makes us realize all the things we have that they never imagined as well as what measure of faith those early pioneers must have had in God!

Sandee Wendler
Sheffield, Iowa

Miscellaneous Meanderings

It's hard to get everyone in the family to agree on a single activity. We started a rotation system where we each pick a reasonable activity and the others must go along. Here are some ideas:

Miniature golf

Hitting a bucket of balls at a driving range

Tourist attractions when there are special offers (last fall we went to the Royal Gorge for a day and spent a morning going up Pike's Peak on the cog railway)

Browsing through antique stores

Free or low-cost outdoor concerts

The Nelson Family
Colorado Springs, Colorado

Daisy Fun

When my children were young we would take a wild daisy and pull off the petals one by one and say, "He loves me, he loves me not" with each petal pulled.

While out driving one day in the country we saw a field of those wild daisies. My three-year-old son spotted the daisies and eagerly shouted, "There's some I love you, I love you nots!"

Betty C. Winterhalter
N. Martinsville, West Virginia

Gotcha!

On a hot day gather up all the water guns, clean shampoo or ketchup bottles, and balloons (to be filled with water), and head outside for a giant water fight. Find a good hiding place, or just sneak up on family members from behind. The wettest person loses!

There's only one rule: No squirting in the face, to avoid damage to the eyes.

Cheryl Cannaverde
Palm Bay, Florida

Their First Fishing Poles

Use inexpensive ice-fishing rods as fishing poles for preschoolers. They will enjoy fishing with these kid-sized, easy-to-pack rods.

Elizabeth Garvey
Howell, Michigan

Sun Tea, Ten Cents!

For those young entrepreneurs who see a need and wish to fill it— adults and parents who don't like lemonade—here's the answer: announcing the first Sun Tea Stand in the neighborhood!

To make sun tea, all you need is a large jar with a lid. Fill with cold water and add at least 3 to 4 tea bags, depending on the size of the jar. Put the lid on and leave jar outside in the sun, preferably on a darker surface to absorb the sun's heat. A few hours is all it takes and then it's business as usual.

Serve with a twist of lemon and maybe a little sugar.

No Job too Small

When our children were between the ages of two and five years old, and always wanted to "help," I would let them "paint." Here's how.

Fill a coffee can with water ("paint"), give children real paintbrushes, and lead them to the outside sidewalk, driveway, or stairs. Children love this activity and there is no mess to clean up!

Debra Kopcio
Belvidere, Illinois

Pajama Run!

Everyone knows children like surprises, so on an evening when all the homework was done and activities were at a lull, I suddenly turned off the television and shouted, "Pajama run!"

Keep in mind the children were in their pajamas and comfortable for the evening. They had no idea what was going on, but it sounded exciting so they played along. I ushered them into the car without letting on exactly what we would be doing.

It wasn't until we were halfway down the block that my oldest began to get serious, asking, "Will we have to get out of the car?" I assured her they would not, so they need not be embarrassed about being out in their pajamas and slippers.

The destination? I pulled into the drive-through lane of a fast-food restaurant and gave their orders for cones or sundaes.

This inexpensive outing had us home in less than fifteen minutes, but the children talked about it for many days. Needless to say, they have let me know since that they're always ready for another "Pajama run!"

Phyllis Moore D'Amico
Clifton Park, New York

The Beat of a Different Drum?

What can you do with empty food or Tupperware containers (with lids), juice cans filled with popcorn kernels (unpopped) with lids taped on, and sandpaper-covered wood pieces? You can get your act together and take it on the road! We're talking drums, maracas, and scrapers for a neighborhood band like no other.

Our kids tried this last summer on the Fourth of July, but you don't need a reason to make music together. At our neighborhood block party adults even joined in with real and really weird instruments.

Here's another tip: If the musicians lose interest, put on a tape and pretend the kids are the percussion section!

Eileen Mollin
New Bedford, Massachusetts

A Wall to China

Did you ever dream on a summer day, while wallowing in the mud in your backyard, what it would be like to create a wall to some distant land? Thinking on a smaller scale, a mud city of your own imagination?

With a little water and plenty of dirt, my kids form mud bricks to bring to life their wildest fantasies! Disposable aluminum baking pans can be used over and over to fashion foundations and bricks.

Bridges, houses, adobe dwellings, and of course, great walls like that one in China are afternoons away!

David Betts and family
Detroit, Michigan

An Underwater Spyscope?

You don't need scuba gear or a fancy face mask to do some primitive underwater exploring as a family. The humble milk carton will do fine, thank you.

Take empty half-gallon milk cartons, rinsed out and dried. Cut off the top and bottom sections of the cartons and stand them on a large piece of plastic wrap. Plastic wrap should be large enough so it can be wrapped up and around the individual cartons and taped inside. Make very sure that the plastic wrap is pulled tightly around the bottom before wrapping up and taping.

Now you're ready for some underwater fun. Place carton gently into water and look inside through the top of the milk carton. Hold carton steady until something swims or floats by...you never know what you'll see!

Taken from "Underwater Spyscope" from Family Fun
Activity Book, *used with permission from Fairview Press,
Minneapolis.* Family Fun Activity Book, *Copyright ©
1994 by Robert Keeshan.*

Winter Ice Cream

Why not use the snow to make ice cream! What you'll need are clean soda cans with tops removed (an adult should do this) and larger containers to put each soda can into; snow (or crushed ice); rock salt; tongue depressors or ice pop sticks; milk, canned milk, sugar, flavorings, and fruits and nuts if desired; and spoons.

Place some rock salt in bottom of larger container and put a soda can in the center. Layer snow and rock salt around soda can until they reach high around the sides. Into each soda can pour 1/2 cup of milk and 1 tablespoon each of sugar and canned milk then add your favorite flavoring. Using the wooden depressor or stick, stir the mixture, being particularly concerned with scraping the freezing ice cream away from the sides of the can so that more milk can be frozen. The mixture is ready to eat when it has reached the consistency of a thick milk shake (about 10 minutes); try adding fruits or nuts for variety. If it's taking too long, add more salt to the snow.

Adapted from **Hug a Tree** *by Robert Rockwell, Elizabeth Sherwood, and Robert Williams. Copyright © 1986: Gryphon House, Inc., Box 207, Beltsville, MD.*

Feed the Birds

Don't buy one from a store! Make a terrific bird feeder from things you have at home and have a fun time building it and your relationship with each other. Then sit back and watch the fun together.

Using a length of thick tree branch, drill holes at various spots in it, fill the holes with suet, and then suspend the log from a tree.

Another suet feeder is made by filling a mesh onion sack with suet, tying it closed, and suspending it from a branch.

Take a clean plastic bleach bottle and cut a hole about 3 inches up from the bottom on each side of it. Thread wire through the neck of the bottle. Fill bottom with seed and hang up in a tree or bush. To protect feeder and seed from the rain and maybe even squirrels, try threading an inverted aluminum pie plate to the top of the bottle before hanging it up.

Adapted from **Hug a Tree** *by Robert Rockwell, Elizabeth Sherwood, and Robert Williams. Copyright © 1986: Gryphon House, Inc., Box 207, Beltsville, MD.*

It's for the Birds

A bird feeder, that is, and one the family can make and then observe the activity of your feathered friends.

Take a large pine cone and tie a string or piece of yarn around the top petals securely. With a spoon or knife, spread peanut butter in all the nooks and crannies of the cone.

Sprinkle birdseed on a sheet of wax paper and roll the peanut butter-covered cone around in the seed. Make sure most of the birdseed gets stuck in the peanut butter.

Hang homemade bird feeder in a tree or another likely bird hot spot.

Sandy Umber
Springdale, Arkansas

Old-Fashioned Girls (or Boys)

Have you ever admired traditional corn husk dolls, often used as part of Thanksgiving table centerpieces? These dolls have been the delight of generations of American children and they're easy and fun to make. In fact, for years my classes at school created these as holiday art projects.

Take three corn husks and, using string, make a knot in the middle. With the knot on top, wrap husks over an old clothespin. With another piece of string, make a knot under pin (at neck). Take brightly colored pipe cleaners to make the doll's arms.

Take several more husks to make either a bouncing skirt or bulky pants, tying in the middle and folding over and tying at the ankles.

Use the reserved corn silk to fashion the doll's hair and then glue in place. Facial features may be painted on with markers. An American tradition continues!

Marie Johnson
Cedar Rapids, Iowa

Plant a Sock

Ever come in from the outdoors and find your socks are covered with seedlike things? Well, some of them probably are seeds and will sprout if you carefully take off the socks and "plant" them. Position a long cake pan at an angle and put some water in its lower end. Drape the top edge of each sock over the top of the pan with the toes of the socks in the water. Place in a warm place where they will receive good light and check every day for new growth. Try planting some of the seedlings and see what they produce.

Adapted from **Hug a Tree** *by Robert Rockwell, Elizabeth Sherwood, and Robert Williams. Copyright © 1986: Gryphon House, Inc., Box 207, Beltsville, MD.*

From Leftovers to Gardens

Don't throw out that carrot top or those potatoes with "eyes"! Keep those grapefruit and apple seeds, those lima beans! They, as well as many other leftovers, can all grow before your very eyes. Here's how.

If working with seeds, put potting soil into each section of a styrofoam egg carton. Plant a seed in each section, keep it moist and give it adequate light, and it will sprout. When large enough for transplanting, plant it outdoors or in a larger container that can be kept inside or out. Some seeds will even sprout if left on a sponge kept damp in a saucer of water.

For a carrot, trim its leaves, cut off the top 2 inches of carrot, and then leave it, cut side down, in a shallow dish with enough water to just cover the carrot. When it forms roots, it can be planted in soil and will produce a fernlike plant. This also works for beet tops.

A potato will produce a pretty vine. Cut a section of potato that contains a growing eye (it will have a white shoot). Insert three or four toothpicks around potato so that it can be suspended in a cup of water so that the cut edge of the potato is kept wet. When there are well-formed roots, plant the potato in soil. A sweet potato can also be used.

When soaked in water for about 15 hours, lima beans will crack open to expose the tiny plant growing inside. Plant a bean and see what happens.

Adapted from The Encyclopedia of Grandparenting *by Rosemary Dalton and Peter Dalton, Copyright © 1992. Used by permission of Bristol Publishing Enterprises, Inc.*

Farmer for a Day

You don't need to own a farm to get those fresh fruits and vegetables for your favorite pies, jellies, or other canned goods. All over the country there are farms that will let you come in (usually for a fee) and pick their fields for the produce you need. Look in the telephone book or call the local extension agency to find out what farms are near you and what produce they have for picking (call before you go to find out their hours and prices as well as directions to the farm). The most common types of produce are fruits such as apples, berries, and grapes and vegetables like peas, beans, squash, and pumpkins.

Dress appropriately and bring along a picnic lunch to make a day of it. Not only will you have farm-fresh food that is great tasting but you will have spent an enjoyable day in the outdoors with your family. Later you can have even more fun making those apple pies, canning those string beans, or making that treasured family recipe for grape jelly or green tomato relish.

The Kite

by Mary Hawkins

I remember feeling very disappointed at the time. Only years later did my city-slicker husband tell me how embarrassed and inadequate he had felt, far more than I realized at the time. The time we tried to make that kite for our three small children.

A new church manse was being built for us so we were living for several weeks in an old house on a farm several miles out of town. One windy day, while roaming the paddocks, I remembered the kites we used to make when I was a kid growing up on our farm.

A rather reluctant husband helped me find two pieces of wood for the cross beam; perhaps they were a little too thick, a little too heavy, but they were all we had. There was plenty of brown paper and plenty of string, glue, and pieces of old material to tie on the tail. There was also an abundance of enthusiasm and small, eager hands.

What there wasn't was plenty of experience in how to tie the string to the kite and how long and heavy to make the tail.

Dreams and memories are wonderful, but don't rely on them to make a kite that will soar high above in the breeze! No matter how hard we ran or how much we adjusted the string and pieces of cloth, our kite never flew.

Twenty-one years later I asked our eldest son what fun family times he remembered the most. Immediately he said, "That time we tried to make a kite."

A failure? Some might think so. But the act of making an inadequate kite did not matter a scrap.

We were a family enjoying each other.

A Tree of Your Own

If your child's school hasn't done this activity, snap it up as an investment in the future of the environment, God's world.

Adopt a tree! Have your child select a tree in your yard or one in a local park and, for your family's purposes only, call it the child's own.

Encourage your child to bring paper and crayons (if very young) in the winter and summer to make bark rubbings. In the fall be sure to press the leaves and save a few. A journal is a good place to record important facts about the tree, such as when the buds appear, when the foliage is full, when the leaves turn, if berries appear, and so on. Be sure to photograph your child at least once a year standing beside the tree. The journals and scrapbooks children keep are wonderful keepsakes of the days of a carefree childhood.

The Fruits of Labor

As a family, in the spring go to a local nursery and have each child pick out their favorite new fruit tree. Set aside a special area of the yard and plant the young saplings. Each child can then care for his or her tree, monitor the tree's growth, and, much later, reap the tasty rewards of commitment!

Janice Schuiling
Holland, Michigan

How Tall Is that Tree?

While this question may seem like one of many riddles parents can't answer, after this activity you'll seem like a genius. Yes, you can be at home in the great outdoors!

How tall *is* that tree? You respond, "I can measure that tree with a twig."

Enlist the assistance of the young inquirer and have him or her stand with his or her back against the tree. After locating a small twig, step back so that you can see the full height of the tree.

Squinting with one eye closed, position the twig so that the top lines up with the top of the child's head. Move your thumb down the twig so that it lines up with the child's feet. Now, move the twig up until your thumb lines up with the child's head. After observing where the top of the twig is in relation to the tree, move your thumb to that place. Making sure to count the number of times you move your thumb to the upper position, continue this procedure until you reach the top of the tree.

Multiply the number of times you jumped up the stick with your thumb by the approximate height of the child. For example, if the child is 4 feet tall and you had to move your thumb up the twig twenty times, you would know the tree is a stately 80 feet tall.

How Old Is that Tree?

As you and your child walk in the woods, be on the lookout for logs and tree stumps. By observing the tree rings, visible only on an exposed piece of wood, you can teach your child how to date a tree.

Each year a tree grows, a new ring of cells is added just under the bark. These cells form passageways that bring water from the roots and sugars from the leaves to the rest of the tree. Observe the light and dark rings: Each light and dark ring together represents one year's growth. The light part is formed in the spring and the dark in the summer. The width of the ring tells if the tree has a good year (wide means good).

As your child counts the annual rings, a story of life emerges, one of good times and bad, the story of a tree.

Flower Power!

In the spring my family enjoys noticing the arrival of all the delightful flowers. Once they could identify the parts of a single blossom, my kids became true garden maniacs. A magnifying glass is not necessary but may make your garden forays more interesting. Here are the flower parts and their various roles:

Petal—the inner floral leaves that invite insects

Sepal—the leafy green outer leaves that serve as a protective shield

Pistil—the female part of the flower, consisting of the seed-bearing ovules in the center of the blossom

Stamen—the male part of the flower, consisting of a slender stalk and a pollen sac

Karen Kambano
Sandyville, Ohio

Home Tweet Home

Discovering where animals or insects live can be an adventurous way in which to give children an appreciation for nature and how living things adapt to their environment and needs.

Take a walk through the woods someday and try to locate some animal homes. Many can be even as close as your own backyard. Look for squirrels' nests, spiders' webs, and birds' nests and notice how they are constructed and the differences between them. When you go to the seashore, observe the small fish and other waterlife that goes in and out with the waves. You might even see something burrowing its way into the sand. Why not stir up some sand gently and see what lives there! Be careful not to harm anything. Continue the lessons and expand your children's little minds even more by referring to books in the library on the particular subjects.

Adapted from **Hug a Tree** *by Robert Rockwell, Elizabeth Sherwood, and Robert Williams. Copyright © 1986: Gryphon House, Inc., Box 207, Beltsville, MD.*

Where Do Things Go at Night?

Ever wonder about that? Well, why not find out! Most children find it an adventure to go out on a night walk through their backyard or neighborhood or a familiar forest trail holding hands with Mom and Dad or their big sister or brother. Dress appropriately and bring flashlights; if walking along roads, wear light-colored clothing or reflective tape or vests. Bring mats to sit on.

Look all around you. As you sweep the beam of the flashlight in front of you, look closely to see eyes reflecting back at you. They might belong to animals, birds, or even a spider. Every once in a while, sit down and listen quietly for sounds and try to identify them. Sprinkle talcum powder over a piece of cardboard and place it in an area that an animal might cross; when it does, there will be tracks that you might be able to identify.

For children afraid of the dark, forget the flashlight and do this during the day just walking or sitting quietly while you look and listen for different animals and insects.

Adapted from **Hug a Tree** *by Robert Rockwell, Elizabeth Sherwood, and Robert Williams. Copyright © 1986: Gryphon House, Inc., Box 207, Beltsville, MD.*

Free Backyard Pets

Toads are smarter than frogs. Snails love to be petted. Ants have their own burial grounds. Ladybugs "leak" orange blood if attacked. Only male crickets can "fiddle."

Collecting insects is one of the surest ways to turn children on to the joys of science and increase their respect for the diversity and interdependence of all creatures in nature. (It's also a great outdoors activity for the whole family and one that can truly stimulate great conversations on the wonders of creation, even the tiniest ones.)

You do need to be patient when catching insects and especially gentle in handling them. Different species can stay together in the same container, if there's enough room and plenty of places for them to hide.

Be aware of what each of your animals is eating. If a lizard or salamander, for example, doesn't eat or appears thinner, return it outdoors so that it can find its natural diet in the wild. Animals with a short life span, such as butterflies, should be kept only a couple of weeks before you release them.

Be safety conscious. Never try to collect wild rodents or snakes. Some ants can sting and a few lizards may bite. Always wash your hands immediately after handling your pets.

Here are some easy, do-it-yourself techniques to help you collect insects:

Beetles, moths, and lacewings: Hang a white sheet from a tree limb, funnel the sheet into a big-mouthed jar, and put a spotlight on the sheet.

Butterflies and grasshoppers: Shape a circle from a wire clothes hanger and fasten the ends to a broom handle with tape or rope. Attach a net made from cheesecloth by sewing it to the wire circle with heavy-duty thread.

Bees and other sweet-loving insects: Paint a tree trunk with molasses or honey.

Earthworms and snails: Make a pile of dead leaves and keep it moist. Best hunting is in the early morning, especially after a light rain.

Frogs: Take a fishing pole (or any long stick) and tie a 3-inch piece of bright cloth (preferably flannel, as the frog's tongue will adhere to the fabric) to the end of the line. Dangle the cloth over the frog, and it will probably flick out a tongue to catch it. You can lure the frog in your direction by moving the line and cloth gradually toward you. Or, if you prefer night stalking, take a flashlight, shine it in the frog's eyes, and sneak a net (or your hand) around from the rear. But don't squeeze too hard, frogs don't like that.

Here is more detailed information on collecting and keeping your backyard pets:

Ants: Look for ant trails near sidewalks and fences. Place sugar, a wet piece of hard candy, or a dead insect on its side near trails; close jar and refrigerate before pouring ants into container. Keep ants in an ant farm (available in toy stores) or a large, 2-quart glass jar. Feed them grass seed, or other small seeds, sugar water (1 teaspoon of sugar in one-half cup water). Ants have separate areas for feeding, sleeping, and burying just like people do.

Butterflies: Find them near flowers on sunny days. Use a butterfly net to catch them. Keep them in a large aquarium with a mesh screen on top; place sticks, grass, and flowers inside. Feed them tubular flowers where nectar is nestled, or any flowers near where they were caught; have sugar water in a pet bottle. (As butterflies do not last long in captivity, they should be released after two weeks.) Some butterflies have "false" eyes to deter predators. Butterflies "taste" with their feet.

Caterpillars: Find them on and beneath various plants such as milkweed, cabbage, tomato, apple, oak, and pine trees. Carefully pick up leaves with caterpillar on them. Keep them in a gallon jar or small aquarium with nylon or mesh screen firmly covering the top. Feed them leaves from the plant near when collected. Watch the metamorphosis as they shed their skin, change into a pupa, and eventually hatch into a moth or butterfly. Many caterpillars feed on toxic substances, such as milkweed, which protects the adults from predator birds.

Crickets: They can be found under stones, in tall grass, near fences. Trap them with a plastic cup, a net, or pick up carefully with your fingers. Keep them in an aquarium or jar covered with nylon stocking or a mesh screen cover; leave an open egg carton or cardboard tube for hiding places. They eat dead insects, bread crumbs, or cereal and can use a wet paper towel for moisture. Crickets can jump more than twenty times their own length; male crickets chirp but female crickets are silent. A cricket's ears are located below the "knee joints" on its front legs.

Earthworms: Find them in damp, loose soil, compost heaps, or on the ground after a heavy rain. Keep them in a small aquarium or large jar with loose, damp soil. Feed them dead and decaying leaves and grass or coffee grounds. If you cover the sides of the earthworm farm with dark paper for a week, when the paper is removed, underground tunnels will be visible next to the glass. Earthworms are both male and female so any two worms of the same species can mate.

Frogs and toads: They can be found in wet, muddy puddles and holes along the edges of lawns and gardens and also in drainpipes. Grasp them firmly but gently from behind or scoop up with a pail. Keep them in any clear, watertight container with 2 inches of soft soil (keep wet); supply a water cup (for frogs to sit in). Feed them crickets, mealworms, or other live insects. Toads and frogs catch insects with a whiplike movement of their tongue. A frog uses its eyeballs to push food down its throat.

Ladybugs: They can be found on roses and other flowers and plants. Brush them into a plastic cup with your hands or break off the leaves they are on. Keep them in a glass quart jar covered with a piece of nylon stocking that is secured with a rubber band. Feed them leaves with small insects on them. Ladybugs can walk upside down on your hand. They do battle with ants that are trying to protect their aphids. They will leak orange blood if they feel threatened by a predator (including a child).

Lizards: Find them near fences, under rocks, and in overgrown areas. Catch them by picking them up gently but firmly from the rear at their midsection. Keep them in a 5-gallon aquarium covered with a screen made of one-quarter-inch wire-mesh (available at hardware stores); place sticks, rocks, and soil inside and spray daily with fine water mist. Feed them mealworms, crickets, beetles, and live insects; some lizards eat flowers and other plants. Lizards like to stalk their prey like miniature dinosaurs. Many lizards have a tail that detaches when grabbed by a predator (or a child).

Newts and salamanders: They can be found under rocks, decaying wood and mulch, or often in muddy holes or ditches. Pick up firmly at the midsection or "herd" into a small container. Keep them in an aquarium with damp sod, rocks, and dead leaves and spray daily with water. Feed them earthworms, live insects, or snails. They will often display color patches if upset or threatened. Salamanders are voiceless; some live up to twenty years. Newts and salamanders have smooth, wet skin; lizards have dry skin.

Snails: Can be found in wet garden plants and around dead leaves. Pick them up firmly by the shell and put in an aquarium with a mesh cover. Feed them dead leaves, grass, and pieces of chalk (for the shell) and spray daily with water. They love to be stroked along the neck (you can tell because they arch it); the tentacles will retract when gently touched. Snails have a flylike tongue and eat their food by scraping it. The shells of snails are made of calcium carbonate, or chalk. Slugs are snails without shells.

Reprinted with the permission of Family Life *magazine, July/August 1994.*

Creepy Vibrations

How about going on a worm hunt? If you ask your kids, chances are they'll look at you in amazement—do you have a fever?—and then they'll agree immediately.

Probably the kids know better than you where the worms hang out in your yard but, if not, here are a few pointers. Find a place where the soil is moist and where you can see worm holes.

This particular method works in the daytime or after dark. All you need are two wooden stakes, a few inches wide, and one of them should have its end sharpened to a point. The other stake should have notches cut along its length deep enough to bump as it slides across the pointed stake.

When you find the right spot in your yard, pound the pointed stake about halfway into the ground. Next, begin pulling the notched edge of the unpointed stake back and forth across the side of the one in the ground, as if you were trying to saw through it. If this is truly a worm zone, worms should begin to crawl out of the ground within five or six minutes after you start "sawing." These are truly creepy vibrations!

Having read that worms cannot find their way home, we asked the kids to carefully direct the worms back to their earthy home.

W. R. Delaney
Prospect Park, New Jersey

Nesting Instincts

Just as your child's room reflects his or her individuality, so a bird's nest is one of a kind as well. My family has participated in the all-important process of nest building by providing nesting materials and then trying to discover the location of "our" nest.

In late spring collect string, paper bits, yarn, felt, and whatever else you think would be appropriate and hang outside on shrubs or trees. Nest building is known to take a week or more so your family has plenty of time to trace the destination of the materials.

Take pictures, keep a journal, and tape record the bird calls— and the calls of new life—as you monitor your co-construction project.

W. R. Delaney
Prospect Park, New Jersey

Gone Fishing

Okay, so you don't subscribe to *Field and Stream*. You can still take your family fishing and actually find a fish. The following list shows some places where fish congregate.

Underwater weed beds	Overhanging trees or foliage
Lily pads	Piers and docks
Merging streams and lakes	Around big rocks
Overarching points of land	Dams and falls

Of course, you don't have to catch the big one to have a great time. Ninety-nine percent of the fun of fishing is just being together, away from the busyness of life.

Anne Ryan
Rochelle Park, New Jersey

I Spy a Spider!

Spiders are our friends, despite the aim of housewives and husbands who diligently swat them down each week.

Introduce your children to the wonder of spiders and their webs. If they have not had the privilege, read them the classic story *Charlotte's Web* by E. B. White as a primer. (Third-grade-age children particularly enjoy listening.)

Spider webs are notoriously easy to find outside. They're usually in such dark musty places as a barn, crawl space, or garage. Look closely to see if the spider is "home." Find a dead bug and try to offer it to the spider.

Observe different kinds of webs. Some are silky, horizontal creations, while others seem like funnels. Have your children sketch the webs found around your yard and look for variations each week. If your family is into photography, try taking pictures of the webs at different times of the day and especially after a rain.

All Eyes Are on You!

If you're outside observing the night sky, you may want to take a late-night walk, especially if you're up on animal eyeshine colors.

Eyeshine colors are those visible when a flashlight is shone on an animal. The following is a list of certain animals' eyeshine colors, ones that you just may encounter:

Frog or toad—green

Raccoon —bright yellow

Skunk—amber

Porcupine—deep red

Fox—bright white

Opossum—dull orange

Meteor Shower!

Every summer there is a two- to three-day period when meteor showers occur. Local newspapers and television usually inform the public when this is going to happen.

As it is vacation time, our children are allowed a middle-of-the-night excursion to witness this celestial event. We wake up around midnight and go outside to watch the falling stars. Lying on our backs in sleeping bags or bundled up in blankets, we look up at the magical sky. If it's chilly, we make hot chocolate and have cookies while we watch.

The late hour—and the beauty of the stars—provides a thrilling family experience.

Leah Dent
Anderson, South Carolina

Ka-Boom!

Because God's universe is filled with so many beautiful wonders one often forgets that the more terrifying occurrences are also gifts from Him. Thunder is a good example.

Did you know that during a typical storm you will begin to hear thunder when the lightning is about ten miles away? In that way, thunder helps people know how far away the storm really is. But there is also a calculation that your kids may find amazing and handy.

To calculate the distance between yourself and a thunderstorm, count the seconds between the time you see a flash of lightning and the time you hear the thunder. Divide the number of seconds by five and the answer is the distance to the storm in miles.

Pictures in the Sky

On a day when a beautiful blue sky is filled with puffy white clouds, lie on the ground with your children and relax. Watch the clouds and have each one tell what the shape of a cloud reminds them of...a bunny, their teddy bear, a car.

On a warm, starry night, lie on the ground and look at the stars and try to see pictures in them. Or bring along a star guidebook and a flashlight and locate the constellations, major stars, and planets.

Watch carefully and you might even see a moving satellite or a shooting star. If the moon is full, try seeing a "picture" in it.

Did you know that on a clear night it's possible to see around a thousand stars? Of course the easiest to recognize is the Big Dipper, which, as its name suggests, resembles a ladle used to serve soup. There are four stars in the "handle" and three around the "ladle." From the Big Dipper it's a short skip to Polaris, most commonly known as the North Star. If you could trace a path from the handle to the ladle and continue it upward you would bump into the bright North Star.

Tell your children they will be following in the footsteps of Christopher Columbus if they can locate the North Star...and they will never be lost.

The pictures of God's universe are truly beyond words!

On the Beach, at Sunrise

On a vacation to the beach with several other families, we found a way to get away as a family and do something special.

Dad woke the entire family early one morning, just before sunrise (everyone was warned in advance!). We had slept in our sweatsuits so we would not have to change. Mom grabbed the picnic basket— prepared the night before—and we all headed to the beach.

Once there we had a short devotion about God's beautiful creation and a prayer time of thanksgiving. As we munched on doughnuts and sweet rolls and washed them down with juice, we knew this activity was a true "memory maker."

Steve and Debbie Barnes
Andersonville, Tennessee

Prepare to Praise

On the way to church we make sure that we have a few tapes of praise songs. These help to get us into the appropriate mood for worship or Bible class. In addition, the songs are especially helpful in calming the tensions that seem to develop as we rush to get ready to go. We started this activity even before we had a cassette player in the car, using a hand-held model.

The Hudgens Family
College Station, Texas

Keeping Sundays Special

My family has made an effort to keep Sundays special. We feel it is vital to reserve a single day out of each week just to be together and worship God.

A special set of rules was applied to the first day of every week, although as children we looked at them as almost luxuries instead of burdens. My brother, sister, and I were not permitted to invite friends over or attend activities. A few exceptions were church gatherings and entertaining people who had traveled from far away for the sole purpose of visiting us. The same regulations are placed on Sundays now, even though I am the only child remaining at home. My parents and I keep Sunday as a day to rest and relax.

A typical Sunday might be as follows. In the morning we attend church and return home around noon. After lunch my parents and I pursue various low-key activities until we are ready for a walk. In the winter our strolls are briefer and closer to home. However, when it is warm we venture into the woods or to a park nearby. We occasionally visit places like Moss Lake, Stoneybrook, or Letchworth. The three of us like pausing to marvel at the beauties of nature in these parks. We bicycle, go on picnics, and, in the past, have visited unusual playgrounds (wooden ones were our favorites).

I have countless memories—both pleasant and appalling—of family adventures in the woods and other places. On one occasion my brother and sister and I were energetically zooming down the pathway when I stepped into a rotten log. What appeared to be huge, terrifying ants with wings were surrounding me. I later learned they were giant black wasps. While at Moss Lake we once discovered a snapping turtle. Near its home we tossed a few bread crumbs into the water. Did that ever get a reaction! Fish were piled on top of one another battling for that bit of food.

As a very small girl I used to fill my pockets with acorns and pine cones. The walks were never boring as I searched for such treasures as unusual stones, pretty leaves, nuts, seeds, flowers, and berries.

My parents always pointed out simple but interesting things for me. We studied frog eggs in a mud puddle, observed a leech in a tiny pool of water, and stopped to listen to old trees creak and groan. Each expedition offered a unique glimpse at nature and gave us a renewed appreciation of life.

Sunday evenings have always been relaxed with no strict schedule. Keeping Sundays special doesn't require extravagant plans or lots of money...only a commitment to your family.

Rachel L. Bell
Shinglehouse, Pennsylvania

Give to Others

One of the most rewarding lessons you can teach your children is how to help others less fortunate than they. Why not take your child to a senior citizens' home and let her talk to or read a magazine article to some of the residents there. Try participating in a neighborhood food collection for the needy. If you need help in locating needy people or organizations, contact your church. If you are already a volunteer, let your child know how good it makes you feel when you are helping others.

With a Smile and a Sheltie?

If your family includes a beloved dog or cat, you may want to volunteer your time in pet therapy.

First, be sure to contact the activities directors of nursing homes or medical centers for permission and clearance. When you visit be as creative as you like. If it's Christmas, why not dress up your pet in holiday costume? Medical personnel across the country agree that pets bring unconditional love to patients without hope, especially those suffering from AIDS and Alzheimer's.

When families come to such care facilities together, their joy, smiles, and laughter—and the warmth of their pet—provide priceless therapy that costs nothing.

The Rev. Juanita Duryea Hilsenbeck
Long Beach, New York

Time Together, for Others

If you're intending to visit nursing homes as a family, gather old magazines ahead of time and bring them with you. Residents never tire of old periodicals.

Other family service projects include cleaning up a park or helping elderly neighbors clean, going shopping, painting, mowing the lawn, and so on.

Sandy Umber
Springdale, Arkansas

A Mitten Ministry

An ongoing fun project for our family is one we call our "mitten ministry."

All year long we stockpile mittens that we find at garage sales or Salvation Army stores. We buy them for a modest price and bring them home to stash in our car.

When the cold weather comes and we see someone braving the outdoors with bare hands, we usually have a pair of mittens that will fit them. Our offering warms both their hands and our hearts.

Lois Rehder Holmes
Havana, Illinois

Scripture on a Starry Night

On a clear night we take our sleeping bags and our favorite snack outside and watch for the first stars to come out. This is a great time to talk about God's wonderful creation and to read selections from Genesis together.

Cheryl Cannaverde
Palm Bay, Florida

Camp under the Stars

After you've gazed at the stars you may want to camp out in the backyard, perhaps on top of a trampoline, on blankets, or in a tent.

Sharon Whitefield
Tolar, Texas

A Love of God, Anytime, Anywhere

As parents we take very seriously the Bible verse, "Teach them to your children talking about them when you sit at home and when you walk along the road, when you lie down and when you get up" (Deuteronomy 11:19, NIV). As you ride in the car together, sit down to watch television, or first wake up in the morning, you should make the most of every opportunity.

These conversations needn't be forced or heavy-handed (we want her to love God, not hate us!). When our daughter remarks about finding some flowers, we might say, "Aren't we glad that God made those flowers so beautiful? He does some pretty awesome work!" Quite often this conversation leads to a deeper thought that only a little person could express.

The Sweet Family
Huntsburg, Ohio

Once Upon a Tent...

Okay, you've embarked on a really fun family adventure, camping in a tent in your own backyard. What happens next?

It's storytime and, as parents, you're the main attraction. Beforehand, try to plan out in your head some possible storylines. Of course, anything that involves your children or somewhere the family has been will be an immediate attention grabber.

But you can also use this as a time for knee-gripping, blood-curdling Bible stories. Look up ahead of time in a children's Bible storybook some possible candidates, then try to visualize the story yourself. Aim for one that doesn't have too many characters and has a fairly simple plot. Don't tell the children right away that this is a story from the Bible; wait until all eyes are glued on you at the end and then reveal that this really, really happened.

Elizabeth Wendlandt
Scottsdale, Arizona

Yard Pards

One of the most treasured times we have is on Saturday mornings when I take my two daughters to yard sales with me. As we scouted the sales for housekeeping items for my son, I was able to teach my daughters good buying habits. (We outfitted his kitchen for around fifty dollars.)

We search the Friday evening paper and make a list of the yard sales in the area and then we follow every sign we see between the ones I have written down. Quitting time is usually around noon. One highlight of the morning is when we stop for a treat. As we eat out infrequently, my daughters really look forward to this.

Pat LeMaster
Greenville, South Carolina

Fair's Fair

When the fair comes to town, watch out! This is one family that thrives on competing in the various activities. I absolutely love entering the photography exhibits. The children enjoy creating works of art for display. All of us have enjoyed raising chickens and entering them for judging. Blue ribbons and Best-of-Show awards have found their way into our joyous little hands many times. The children thrill in discovering what they have won and are proud to have their own creations and hard work displayed for all to seé.

Lisa D. Hughes
Phoenix, Arizona

One on One

My three children were all born less than three years apart, and because of their closeness in age I had trouble finding time to spend with each one, one on one. A friend and I then began trading off Fridays for a "mother's morning out" time.

On my particular Friday, I will take one of my children out on a "date." The date consists of going to a place of their choice and doing whatever they want. We might go to the toy store at the mall and take an hour to look at toys or to the pet store or park. My only rule is that we never buy anything at a store; we just enjoy looking. Afterward we go to a fast-food restaurant (of their choice) and get a children's meal. I can't afford to buy meals for all of my children at once so this is an added treat. We then will stop by the grocery store or dollar store and choose small surprises for the two children who have not been with us.

This individual time has helped our relationships grow and develop beyond measure. Children learn the joy of giving as well as they choose the small surprises for their siblings; the siblings, on the other hand, learn socialization skills with the other children.

Kimberly Wentworth
Colbert, Georgia

Camp Volunteers

There is a Bible camp a few hours from our home and my husband often volunteers his time there to do new construction work. As there are no campers on the premises, we go as a family and spend a few days. My son and I enjoy the camp facilities while my husband works, and then we spend the evenings doing things together.

Margaret Heckman
Mayville, Michigan

Enough Coins for a Picnic

One day when the kids kept saying, "Let's go somewhere, let's go somewhere!" and our funds had run low, we raided the family coin jar and went for a drive.

On our way we passed a small roadside park. We drove a little farther and, after we turned around, we stopped at a small store and counted our change. There was enough for a loaf of bread, a package of ham, chips, and soda pop. We stopped at the park, ate, and explored the area. What a fun way to spend a few hours together!

Debbie Santonia
Seth, West Virginia

Walk with Me

An activity our family has come to enjoy is hiking. Not only will you be getting great exercise, this is an activity all ages of children can enjoy.

Look at information centers and state and national parks for hiking spots near you. Then take the family and enjoy being together in God's creation, near mountains, streams, or waterfalls. We usually pack a picnic so that our only expense is the cost of gas.

The Cape Family
Royston, Georgia

Saturday in the Park

With our young family we like to plan activities that are simple and close to home. This past summer we made a habit of going on family picnics every Friday and/or Saturday evening.

We prepare all the food at home. Dinner entrees have included hot dogs, hamburgers, chicken, or sandwiches, with crackers, fruit, and cookies for dessert. The parks, which were within a ten-minute drive of home, sometimes had a walking trail but always had a playground.

The idea is that once you get to the park everything is ready to serve and enjoy, and that gives you more time to enjoy being with your family. One additional benefit: Spending that time at a park kept at-home projects from interfering!

Mark and Ann Goetz
Tecumseh, Michigan

Cool Off

Going out for ice cream cones at the local snack bar was our family's treat for years, but as prices went up and the size of cones went down, we felt the need for a change in tradition.

We now head for the supermarket with our small cooler, spoons, napkins, and bowls (or a box of cones). There we buy a half-gallon of ice cream and dish it out at a local park or while on a scenic drive. The price is right, we get as much ice cream as we like, and the rest goes into the cooler to take home.

Andy and Gayle Alexson
Dixfield, Maine

No Picnic Is Complete. . .

...without roasted apples (oh, and don't forget the hot dogs, raw veggies with dip, and plenty of lemonade). Here's the recipe.

Remove the core from each apple, leaving the bottom skin intact. Pack the core with a mixture of brown sugar and cinnamon. Wrap each apple in aluminum foil and place in the coals of the campfire at the beginning of your meal. By the time everyone is finished eating, your apples will be soft and ready to enjoy.

The Schafer Family
Sycamore, Ohio

Treasure Hunt in the Park

While enjoying a picnic at a state park, have a treasure hunt. Our family hunts for such articles as nuts, pine cones, different leaves, a soda can, different out-of-state license plates, pens and pencils, newspaper, and other items.

Mildred J. Switzer
St. Thomas, Pennsylvania

King Mac's and Wendy's Kentucky Fried Fiestas?

Or how to have a progressive dinner at your favorite fast-food restaurants!

Decide as a family which restaurants you will frequent. Eat french fries at one, hamburgers at another, drinks somewhere else, and top it all off with dessert at yes, another establishment.

Betty B. Robertson
Roanoke, Virginia

To Take Out or Go Out?

That is the question. Whether 'tis nobler to suffer the consequences of irritable, tired, and hungry toddlers in the privacy of one's home, or enjoy the pleasures of dinner by candlelight with stimulating conversation and no dishes?? Apologies to Shakespeare, but everyone needs a break from cooking now and then, and you have to decide whether your family is ready for a dining-out experience. The following is a guide to the types of restaurants and appropriate manners that should be noted at each. If good manners are properly addressed when children are small, as they mature dining out becomes even more pleasurable and relaxing for everyone.

Fast-food restaurants are definitely kid-friendly and may be the best first dining-out experience for your family. Even in such establishments be sure to stress the importance of good manners, especially "please" and "thank you" and cleaning up after you finish by disposing of all food materials and papers.

Cafeterias can be a fun experience since there are always more choices than family members can possibly eat. At such a place, remind kids that their eyes are usually bigger than their stomachs.

One step higher toward finer dining are so-called family restaurants where food is brought to the table by waiters and waitresses. Silverware if wrapped in a napkin should be positioned correctly upon sitting and napkins should go on laps. Empty cracker papers or butter wrappings should go in the ashtray or under dinner plates. Never summon a waiter or waitress by tapping a glass, snapping fingers, clapping hands, or whistling. Address them as "waiter" or "waitress."

When salad bars are provided, remember never to use fingers to procure an item, especially bread and rolls. Avoid spilling the contents of the various salads.

A gourmet restaurant doesn't necessarily mean a better restaurant than those mentioned above. Obviously, it's more expensive and requires that diners wear dressier clothes than they might to more family-oriented establishments. If there are items on the menu family members don't understand, encourage them to ask the restaurant's staff to explain them. Kids usually enjoy doing this as they feel especially grown up. At such a restaurant, you can and should expect excellent service and your manners should be exemplary as well. If silverware is dropped on the floor, leave it and ask for a replacement. A tip of at least 15 percent is customary if service and food have been appreciated.

Adapted from The Family Book of Manners *by Hermine Hartley (Barbour and Company, Inc., 1990).*

The Family Picnic

by Mary Hawkins

I would imagine that most authors find that personal memories of family life trigger ideas for scenes and backgrounds in their stories. This has certainly been the case for me. As they read my novels, my mother, sister, and brothers smile at familiar settings and background snippets that have crept into the stories. Two of my inspirational romances, *Search for Tomorrow* and *Search for Yesterday*, are set mainly on the black soil plains of the Darling Downs in Queensland where I grew up.

My father had a special love and concern for family. Perhaps this was because he and my mother had moved so far from their own families in South Australia. However, over several years his parents, brothers, and three cousins and their families also moved to the Darling Downs. As the Pedler family grew, the best way for all of us to see each other was at family picnics. Photos and home movies of those times are treasured today. These picnics often involved a game of "rounders," a family fun perversion of cricket, baseball, and softball with our own rules!

Almost all our picnics were held on the banks of a creek or dam. Such locales were many miles away across the treeless plains from our farms. Only there did the tall river gums provide shade on scorching summer days. Usually there was enough water still in the creek to find a waterhole big enough to cool off in after the game of rounders.

And the food! I still remember the sausage rolls, chicken,

lamingtons, fruit cake, and the huge watermelons. Only now do I appreciate the hard work and planning that my mother and the other women put into those days. The men often had to make the sacrifice of putting off work on the farm. The Family Picnic had top priority!

Copyright © 1995 by Mary Hawkins.
Mary Hawkins is a widely published author of inspirational romance who makes her home in New South Wales, Australia.

The Book of Family Fun

celebrations

**God has provided us with family and friends. . .
but, most of all, He has given us His Son.**

Celebrate Your Family

Every year, on a designated Sunday, have a special celebration just for your family. Dress up, set the table with your best linens and dishes, and serve your favorite foods. During dinner have each member tell the benefits of being in the family and what they think is wonderful about each family member. Finish off with a great dessert and then sit around the table while looking at the pictures in family picture albums and reminiscing about the good times you've had together.

Childhood Memories

One fun, exciting, and inexpensive way to make a wonderful family memory is to celebrate a holiday as a family.

For several years we have watched the fireworks on the Fourth of July. Both the kids and parents have enjoyed this and it has been a happy memory for us. When we celebrated New Year's Eve, it, too, was memorable. We stayed up until midnight and went outside with confetti poppers.

Celebrating Christmas over the years has been very enjoyable and something to reminisce about in the future. I have been able to remember ever since I was small being with my grandparents, aunts and uncles, cousins, great-aunts, and so on and driving around in the van looking at Christmas lights and singing Christmas carols. Of course I loved receiving Christmas presents but what I remember more are the loving things we did together as a family. I will remember things like decorating the tree together more than I will ever remember what presents I received and from whom.

Elizabeth E. Johnston
(age 14)
Odessa, Texas

The 200,000-Mile Party

In appreciation for God's supply of our first brand-new car, our family dedicated this new set of wheels to Him. Several years later when this car rolled over 200,000 miles, we had a 200,000-mile party!

In white shoe polish were written the words "200,000 miles—PTL" on the car windows. The family drove from restaurant to restaurant to celebrate with a progressive dinner. Dessert was enjoyed with friends at church after the midweek service.

Over one year later while dining at another restaurant a waitress recognized us as the family who praised God for keeping an old car running.

Lynn Sansone
St. Peters, Missouri

A Green Theme

When our children were young, we would celebrate St. Patrick's Day with green food—green pancakes, green applesauce, and so on. We would even invite our children's grade school classes over for lunch (we lived two houses from the school).

Nancy Morast
Kalispell, Montana

School's Out!

Our family celebrates the last day of school. Since that day ends before noon, we take our boys out for lunch, then fill the afternoon with a variety of activities. In the past we've played miniature golf, gone to the dollar theater or window shopping, or sampled foods at a supermarket. Later, after a simple dinner, we indulge in a special dessert to congratulate our students on a job well done. Grandma has even joined us for the fun!

Sara Everett
Hesperia, California

The Old Red, White, and Blue

For Independence Day (the Fourth of July) have everyone in your family wear a patriotic set of clothes (all red, white, and blue). Make sure you choose the items a day or two ahead so they will be washed and ready. Use the opportunity to explain the significance of the colors. Everyone will get into the spirit!

The Hudgens Family
College Station, Texas

Brother's/Sister's Day

Our children enjoy making gifts and celebrating Mother's Day and Father's Day for us. A few years ago, however, they decided to start Brother's Day and Sister's Day. They chose their own dates and made the days memorable for each other by making gifts and special treats.

Kathryn Bechtel
Muncy Valley, Pennsylvania

Honor Your Grandparents

In October, for Grandparent's Day, make a special visit to elderly members of your church or neighborhood as a family. It can be an extended event if you spend time making cookies or other treats beforehand. Encourage the kids to draw pictures or write notes to these special people. A trip to a residence or nursing home can be especially noteworthy at this time. These activities encourage very rewarding relationships between your family and the "adopted" grandparents.

The Hudgens Family
College Station, Texas

Welcome Home, Daddy!

Here's a celebration of a different kind...to honor a special family member after a particularly difficult week.

We started preparations for our "Welcome Home, Daddy" party by baking a heart-shaped cake, along with six cupcakes. We blew up balloons and scattered them everywhere. A "Welcome Home" banner was made and thumb-tacked to the bannister around the porch, along with balloons on each side so that he could see them when he drove up. My daughter and I wrapped a couple of small gifts; she was particularly thrilled with the idea of a party with all the trimmings. She also painted her daddy a picture that she proudly presented to him when he walked through the door.

When Daddy finally arrived he was overwhelmed by the attention. He even forgot for a while life's stresses and felt like the admired special father that he is.

Karen Arrowood
Christiansburg, Virginia

A Co-birthday Celebration?

My sons were born on the same day, four years apart. Celebrating birthdays and scheduling various parties became especially difficult. Why not have a co-birthday celebration?

We reserved the baseball field at a park by a lake and invited all our relatives and friends to a casual game of softball. The kids competed against the adults!

Laughs were had by everybody as less-than-agile fathers tried to impress the boys with their rusty skills and even grandpas joined in the game. Younger boys felt no pressure to be athletic when they watched some of their truly uncoordinated mothers. The highest recommendation? "Same time, next year."

Naomi Shibata
Poway, California

What Is Your Pleasure?

On birthdays we always let the honored family member choose the menu for the dinner celebration. Of course, the birthday boy or girl is not required to help in either the preparation or cleanup, a real reason to celebrate!

While enjoying a wonderful feast with family and friends, we often go around the table and share a poignant or humorous memory that we have of the person over the past year.

Another nice touch is to create a memory centerpiece on the table, including a potpourri of items that bring to mind that family member. We have included such disparate items as ticket stubs from local plays, school art projects, favorite flowers, favorite (small) stuffed animals, miniature sports equipment, baseball cards, and so on. Everyone participates, thus making the centerpiece more meaningful.

Brenda Cordes
Mahwah, New Jersey

When I Was Your Age...

Whether or not you're blessed with an extended family nearby, you can make birthdays truly a family affair. When a birthday of one in your immediate family is approaching, start a phone or letter chain to place an order for family memories.

Here's what we do. We request from grandparents, great-aunts and uncles, cousins, and so on their written or recorded memories from when they were the upcoming age of a family member. To spark their memories, we sometimes include a few questions: What was your favorite subject in school? What sports did you play? Who were your heroes? What songs did you like? What were your future plans? Make sure their answers are on hand for the birthday celebration where they will be read with great delight!

If a relative who lives a distance away is having a birthday and we can't be present, we like to send them a birthday box! We include everything suitable for their special day and, of course, a tape of us crooning our best rendition of "Happy Birthday."

Linda Warner
Uhrichsville, Ohio

When You Were Little

During a family birthday party have each person recall something wonderful or funny about the birthday person. Or pull out their baby book and read parts of it. Then sit back and enjoy all the other memories that are bound to be shared.

This Is Your Life

When my husband turned thirty-five years old he came home from work as usual. But when he entered through the door of our home, the routine stopped.

Our three daughters tackled and blindfolded him and then led him to the passenger's seat of our car. We launched out on a memory tour of my husband's life.

When we arrived at the first destination the girls removed the blindfold and, voilà! My husband faced a building that had been the hospital where he was born. Cameras snapped. The next stop was his first home, then his grade school. Let the record show that my husband thought the halls were much bigger. Another photo session was held. Back in the car, we drove to the "corner" where he and his friends met every evening (yes, another "Kodak Moment"). We continued to the pizzeria where he had his first job, his high school and college, the restaurant where we had our first date, and the hospital where he was first employed full-time.

We visited all the memorable places of a wonderfully full life, and our daughters can now associate these places with their father's stories.

Lynn Sansone
St. Peters, Missouri

Dad's Day

One rainy day during summer vacation the kids were bored with being inside. However, this day also happened to be their father's birthday. What to do?

As a stay-at-home mom I always wanted to take my husband out on his special day but couldn't afford to unless he paid for it, which didn't seem quite right. On this particular day I decided to take him out *and* give the kids something special and fun to do.

We turned our family room into a restaurant. Not only that, we cooked his favorite foods, decorated the room appropriately, and later the kids dressed up as waiter, waitress, and hostess as a certain couple arrived for dinner.

This idea has grown over the years. The first time we did a country inn theme with swiss steak, salad bar, potatoes, and dessert, all by candlelight. The next year we had a sports theme and dubbed our restaurant The Locker Room. The kids wore referee shirts and caps (any sports uniform would work) and we fixed burgers and onion rings. Choose your favorite restaurant—Mexican, Italian, barbecue—and then use your imagination!

Leah Dent
Anderson, South Carolina

Your Day

Wedding anniversaries can be celebrated by the entire family. Sometime during the week before our anniversary our children ride their bikes to a nearby store and use their allowance money to purchase the items required for the dinner...be prepared!

On the day of the dinner, the children spread out one of their mother's better tablecloths, break out the china (figuratively, of course!), and place candles and flowers on the table. They don aprons and are in control of the kitchen for the remainder of the evening. Dinners usually include some type of appetizer, a marvelous salad, the main entree, and they never forget dessert. A bottle of nonalcoholic grape juice has usually been purchased and our son enjoys pouring the first small glass for me to sample. Our daughter is right there, refilling our water glasses and asking if there's anything else she can get for us.

This wonderful evening gives the children the opportunity to show their love in a special, meaningful way without breaking their budgets.

The Mergos Family
Southfield, Michigan

A Sleepover like No Other

For girls, ages ten to fifteen, a sleepover is the birthday party of choice. Here are some special touches you may want to consider to make your daughter's evening even more memorable.

When guests arrive, give each one a men's T-shirt. Provide an assortment of colored, permanent markers to use for coloring the shirts. Put a folded paper grocery bag inside the T-shirt so that the marker doesn't go through. The girls can draw their names or a picture or write "Kellie's Sleepover" (inserting the guest of honor's name). Encourage them to sign one another's shirts. These party favors will go home with the girls.

Serve pizza for dinner, the health food of the evening! If you start the party after dinner, make snack food sculptures. Provide four or five different kinds of snack foods such as potato chips, corn chips, pretzels, nacho chips, popcorn, and so on. You will also need three 8-ounce packages of cream cheese, 8 ounces of sour cream, one package of dried onion soup mix, a mixing bowl, and a spoon and plastic knives. Prepare the paste before the party. (Mix the cream cheese and sour cream and stir in a package of the soup mix.) The edible paste will be used to stick the sculptures together.

Divide the kids into groups or let them work alone. Give each group or girl a paper plate on which to hold her sculpture. Have contests for the tallest sculpture, the most creative, the one that looks the least like school, and so on. Afterward, let them dig in!

Before you resort to board games or videos, here are two games to encourage friendship and fun.

Human knot—Players join hands and form a circle. Two players stand away from the circle and close their eyes. The players in the circle twist themselves into a large knot by going over, under, around, and through the other players, without breaking hands. After a good knot has been formed, the two players outside of the circle open their eyes and try to figure out how to untangle the group. Cooperation is the key, and of course lots of laughter.

Laser light—Darken the room as much as possible. Choose one player to be the space patrolperson and stand guard over the space station in the middle of room (on a chair) with her laser light (flashlight). The person who is the guard covers her eyes and counts to fifty while everyone hides. The object of the game is to get to the space station in the center without getting tagged with the flashlight beam. If a player gets caught, she is instantly frozen in space until the game ends. The first person to get to the space station without getting caught is the next space patrolperson.

Adapted from **Parties with a Purpose**
by Karol Ladd (Thomas Nelson Publishers, 1993).
Used with permission by the publisher.

Lights, Action, Videos!

Kids of all ages love movies, and Christian parents have a special responsibility to make sure all "film fodder" is pleasing to the Lord. Not an easy task these days!

Focus on the Family's McGee and Me film series, for example, is recommended for kids in grade school through middle school. [Editors' note: *The Movie Reporter, How to Choose a Good Video Every*

Time by Phil Boatwright (Barbour Books, 1993) is a good resource for parents when selecting videos for themselves and their children.]

You can't go wrong with a movie party if you've got the right videos. To announce such an event, you might consider making a video invitation. You'll need a camcorder and willing participants (your child and maybe one or two friends) who issue the invite in their own crazy way. Make sure the video is distributed to all invited.

When guests arrive, hand them each a pair of sunglasses, essential equipment for any movie mogul. Provide plenty of snack foods ("Let's do lunch") and hand each guest a review sheet for their movie review.

If you have time before the movies begin, here's a fun acting game to get your guests into the spirit of Hollywood. Divide the group into two teams by counting off. The object of the game is for players to transform as quickly as possible into whatever object you describe. Call out the name of an object and team members must arrange themselves into that shape. If you say "jumbo jet," for example, the players must decide who will be the wings, cockpit, body, and tail. Other ideas include a forest, balloons, a house, bus, or church. The adults present are the judges.

Adapted from **Parties with a Purpose**
by Karol Ladd (Thomas Nelson Publishers, 1993).
Used with permission by the publisher.

A Gift of Love

When our son and daughter-in-law left the United States for the mission field, joining them, of course, was our two-year-old grandson who is very close to us. We were well aware that we were going to miss them very much, and that little Peter would miss his family in the U.S.

Consequently, I subscribed to a children's magazine that I had been reading to my grandson each month. As I receive the magazine, I record portions of it on cassettes, and I also make additional comments. I mail the tapes and the magazine to him each month.

Peter loves receiving the magazine and he loves hearing Grandma's familiar voice! He knows that when I say "Ding," it's time to turn the page.

Verna Bennett
Sumner, Illinois

While Daddy's Away

When my husband was in the Air Force, we looked for a fun way to keep father and daughters close during the frequent separations. We finally hit upon a way that could have many variations (it could also work for mommies who go away).

Before he left we would secretly videotape him talking to them, taping a segment for each day that he would be gone. In each segment he would also show them where to look for a little surprise hidden away for them. The surprises ranged from inexpensive gifts and yummy goodies to such things as coupons for a special date with Daddy when he returns. They had a ball watching their "Daddy Video" and dashing around to find that day's prize. It also made the separation seem much shorter.

Bonnie Sherwood
Kenai, Alaska

To Love and Cherish

A scavenger hunt plus messages of love equals Valentine's Day at our house!

Every family member makes homemade valentines for everyone. We then hide our valentines around the house and later we search to find ours. These precious valentines are truly personalized: Each one expresses why that family member appreciates you.

We have saved all our valentines in airtight bags to be read later in the year when we need a boost of love.

Connie Jurisch
Baldwin, Wisconsin

From the Heart

To make our homemade valentines, we use a variety of materials such as recycled aluminum foil, construction paper, glitter, and doilies.

Onto each valentine we may glue an old key and write the words, "You have the key to my heart." Sometimes we glue a penny and write "I wouldn't be worth a penny without you." Plastic googly eyes have been known to be glued on with "I have eyes for you."

Whatever the heartfelt sentiment, be creative.

Kelly Arvidson
Fosston, Minnesota

Love Box

Decorate a large-sized box and a few weeks before Valentine's Day have each family member start to fill it with anonymous love notes about other family members. The notes could tell of a good deed that person did or describe how wonderful that person is. On Valentine's Day, with the family sitting around the dinner table, have each person pick out one note and read it aloud. Continue to do this until the box is empty.

A Love Tree

Take a branch from a tree or bush and put it in a vase of water. Cut out a supply of red paper hearts. Punch a hole into each heart at its top center; thread yarn or narrow ribbon through each hole and tie closed. Using as many hearts as necessary, write the name of a person or thing that you love and hang the hearts from the tree. Leave hearts and pen next to vase so that everyone can add their "loves" to the tree.

Love Chain

If members of your family are scattered all over the country, here's an economical way to make sure each is wished a "Happy Valentine's Day," or "Merry Christmas," and so on. Distribute a list of people to be contacted and have a phone chain to express the sentiments for that day. The "starter" of the chain could always be the same person or could be selected on a rotating basis.

Picture Cookies

Make large, round sugar cookies and, using colored icings, draw a red rose, a heart, or another valentine symbol onto the cookie. When dry, put the cookie into a plastic bag and tie it closed with a fancy red ribbon.

Valentine's Vittles

Although anything red or heart-shaped will do, here are some other suggestions for picture-perfect Valentine's Day meals.

Make up a vegetable or fruit platter using just red or white vegetables or fruits such as radishes, cherries, strawberries, cauliflower, cherry tomatoes, red apples or grapes, sweet red peppers, peeled cucumbers, and fresh mushrooms.

For valentine sandwiches, start by cutting the bread into heart shapes using a heart-shaped cookie cutter. Fill with cream cheese and pimiento or make toasted cheese sandwiches using tomato slices and white American cheese.

Make a heart-shaped pizza. When stretching out the dough, make it into a heart shape. Proceed as usual, topping it with the red pizza sauce and mozzarella cheese. If you cannot stretch the dough into a heart shape, spread the sauce and cheese into a heartshape.

For a dessert, put vanilla ice cream, yogurt, or pudding into long-stemmed glasses and top with red berries. Or make a heart-shaped cake. If you do not have a heart-shaped pan, bake half the mixture in an 8-inch-round cake pan and the other half in an 8-inch-square pan. When done, cut the circular layer in half. With square layer positioned like a diamond, place cut circular halves against two adjoining edges of the square. Use white and red frostings and decorations to finish the cake.

For a beverage, serve tomato juice or another red juice, such as cranberry, either plain or mixed with another favorite juice.

*A family celebration can mean a celebration of love...
between a husband and a wife.*

Culprit

by Patsy J. Clairmont

I had never kidnapped anyone before, and I was quite excited at the prospect. All the details had to be set in motion if I were to pull it off. This would require accomplices.

I called my victim's workplace, and the secretary (alias the boss's wife) agreed to schedule a bogus meeting for the employees on Friday at noon.

Next, I lined up my mom to stay at the house with Jason while I was on the lam. I then packed a suitcase, smuggled it to the car, and stashed it in the trunk.

I included only a few conspirators to help prevent a leak that would blow this whole operation. I didn't need a traitor; I had too much riding on this to let someone squeal and mess up my action.

A couple of hours away from the scene of the crime was a hotel. I called the innkeeper and told him to get things ready and to make sure I wasn't disturbed after I arrived. I promised him if he followed instructions I'd make it worth his while.

Finally the day arrived. My heart was racing with anticipation. Everything was going as planned.

I arrived at the victim's workplace at 12:01. Entering the front door, I asked him if I could speak to him for a moment in my car.

I had left the engine running and, when he got in and closed the door, I sped off.

At first there were verbal objections. "You can't do this! You can't do this!"

I handed him a hand-scrawled statement.

Dear Husband,

You have just been officially kidnapped. All necessary people have been notified. All business matters have been covered. Your clothes are in the trunk. Take a deep breath. Relax. I'm in charge now, and you must do as I say.

Love,
Patsy

We arrived at the Victorian bed and breakfast, which was decorated for the holidays. We had our picture taken in old-fashioned garb to commemorate my crime. I showered him with gifts—a shirt, pants, robe, and slippers. I purchased a tape of old funny radio

celebrations

broadcasts. We reminisced and giggled and had a wonderful time.
    I wonder if this would be considered a crime of passion? If so, I
plead guilty.

Excerpt from **God Uses Cracked Pots** *by Patsy Clairmont.*
Copyright © 1991, Patsy Clairmont. Used by permission
of Focus on the Family.

May Baskets

Spring's finally here and those first flowers are starting to come up.
Celebrate May Day—May first—by making traditional May baskets.
Using construction paper, make a cone and staple a handle across
its top. Fill with beautiful flowers or grasses and candies and hang
on a neighbor's door handle. Then ring the doorbell and run and
hide as you watch the inevitable expressions of surprise and delight.
Happy May Day!

Elizabeth Wendlandt
Scottsdale, Arizona

Follow that Rabbit!

The night before Easter, we make rabbit tracks leading to the hidden baskets. In the morning, we watch gleefully as our children
follow the tracks to their baskets. To make the tracks, dip your fingers in flour and "stamp" the tracks onto the floor. The children
later pretend they're the Easter Bunny and create their own rabbit
trail.

Amy Mollin
New Bedford, Massachusetts

A Child's Most Important Decision

Why are the biggest family celebrations those that surround graduations or weddings? Doesn't a child's faith decision and entry into the church merit a celebration? (Besides, they may never marry or graduate.)

The evening before a baptism we invite grandparents, aunts, uncles, and cousins, our pastor, and a few friends from church. The house is decorated with flowers and balloons and photos are taken continuously.

The guest of honor is later given a photo album to fill with his or her choice of pictures from the party.

Kjersti Baez
Ossining, New York

Heirloom Gown

A wonderful tradition to have within a family is to pass down a beautiful family christening gown from child to child, generation after generation. To honor each baby christened in the gown (as well as to keep a record of the events), embroider each name and date of ceremony in an inconspicuous spot, such as the hem of the dress or the slip, if there is one. After each ceremony, carefully clean and store the gown so it will be ready for your grandchild or great-grandchild.

Therese Cerbie
Harrington Park, New Jersey

A Circle of Prayer and Hope

At home after a dedication ceremony position everyone, standing or sitting, in a circle and carefully pass the baby from one person to the other. As each person holds the baby, have him or her say a prayer, out loud or silently, to the baby for a safe and meaningful journey through life.

Is It a Memory?

Oh, those sounds and coos of a newborn are so precious that you wish you could hold on to them forever!

Keep a special tape ready in a nearby tape recorder and tape those sounds whenever they occur. Have the tape recorder and tape in a room, such as the kitchen, where you spend the most time talking to your baby. And don't stop recording once the baby is beyond infancy. An audio record of your child (including your conversations) as he or she learns to speak will provide great fun as you both listen to the tapes in later years. Remember to date the tapes and keep in a safe place.

Therese Cerbie
Harrington Park, New Jersey

Special Thanks

As you grow older you tend to realize all that your parents did for you while you were growing up. For the next Mother's or Father's Day or a day in-between write a truly sincere letter thanking one or both for all they did for you.

Take a trip down memory lane and thank them for all the times they cleaned your scraped knees, all the places they took you, all the times they helped you with your homework, all the good values they instilled in you. Try to remember those special, once-in-a-lifetime events when, as always, your parents were there for you. Like when you broke your leg or the time you weren't invited to your so-called best friend's birthday party or when they helped you put together your science experiment for your eighth-grade science fair at school.

Frances Shanahan
Williamsville, New York

For Older Parents

As your parents grow older, it becomes increasingly difficult to find just the right Mother's or Father's Day gift for them because they have all they need. Instead of giving a tangible present, why not give them a gift of service. Promise to do a particular chore for them that they have difficulty doing. Mow the lawn, wash the windows, paint their bedroom, or fix something that is broken...that leaky faucet, the broken window, the gutter that's falling off the garage. And while you're there, remember to stop and celebrate your time together.

Gifts from the Children

Before Mother's Day or Father's Day comes around, the parent not being celebrated can help the children get a gift for the parent being honored. Although there are the usual items that can be given, such as a box of candy or a sweater, here are some suggestions for more personal gifts.

Give the parent being honored the day off to go somewhere and do what he or she wants. Perhaps pack a picnic lunch that he or she can eat while resting on a beach or lying on the grass in a favorite park. Remember to include a book that he or she has been wanting to read. If you want to do more while the parent is away, have the rest of the family do chores of love such as wash, fold, and put away the laundry, mow the lawn, clean up the workroom, and so on.

Honor the parent with a great dinner, made specially for him or her and including favorite foods. After dinner, have each family member give a speech on a special event in that parent's life or just relate why that person is so special and so dearly loved.

The Un-Halloween

Since we decided as Christian parents not to participate in Halloween activities, including trick or treating, we came up with alternative festivities so that our children would have fun and receive candy in a godly way.

For each child make up a set of Bible verse clues. The children have to look up the Scripture text and within that text find the clue to the location of the treat. When they find the treat, there they'll find the next Bible verse clue leading to the next treat.

You may want to color code the clues so the children won't stumble over another's treats and clues.

We used verses with such phrases as "the bread of life" or "living water": The treats for these would be found, respectively, where we kept the bread and in a shower or sink area. Make your clues difficult or easy depending on the child's Bible knowledge.

Your children will be receiving the Word of God, and becoming more familiar with their Bibles, while not feeling left out of the Halloween activities.

Leah Dent
Anderson, South Carolina

The Least of These

Sometime during the Thanksgiving or Christmas holiday seasons, think about giving to people who are needier than you. During a regular grocery shopping trip, buy extra food and then donate the food basket to a local charity, a homeless shelter, or ask your church to give items to a needy family. Have your children partake in the process so they can learn how wonderful it feels to give, rather than receive. Perhaps they have a favorite charity as well.

Feathers and More Feathers

At the beginning of November we use construction paper to make a turkey's head and a supply of feathers for him. We then glue the head to the center of a piece of white posterboard. Names for the turkey are suggested and voted on.

As a family, we use the turkey and feathers to remind ourselves about a Native American custom where some tribes would give feathers to the children for the good deeds they had done. With our version when a child does a good deed Mom or Dad writes the deed on a feather and gives it to the child who then glues it to the turkey. By Thanksgiving the turkey has so many feathers that he appears to be very fat and colorful.

This activity not only helps the child feel good but it opens the parents' eyes to how many positive things the children are doing.

Cathie Orozco
College Station, Texas

Feather Your Nest

At Thanksgiving we cut out feather shapes from construction paper. On these shapes family members write what they are thankful for. We then hide the feathers around the house and have a "feather find." (Sometimes we have to play "hot and cold" to determine the hiding spots.)

The most important thing is to emphasize how truly blessed we are as a family.

Kelly Arvidson
Fosston, Minnesota

Have a "Home for the Holidays" Meal

This traditional Thanksgiving dinner is flavored with the fun of all the family helping with the preparation and planning. This meal can be adapted for any family, regardless of the ages of the members. Here's how you can truly be home for the holidays.

Depending on the ages of the children, write or draw pictures on slips of paper of the main dishes of a Thanksgiving dinner: appetizers, beverages, relish tray, bread, salad, vegetable, turkey and dressing, potatoes and gravy, and desserts. In addition, include on separate slips special tasks involved in the preparation and clean-up of the meal: setting the table, clearing the table, putting food away, loading the dishwasher or washing dishes, scrubbing pots and pans, and putting away dishes.

Each person should select at least one slip from the food group and one from the preparation pile. Whatever food is selected, that person must decide what to serve for that course. Don't be surprised if your four year old chooses chocolate chip cookies instead of pumpkin pie for dessert! That's what makes memories, and what creates a fun family activity. Once the choices are made, the ingredients are then compiled for the shopping list.

Each year the complete Thanksgiving meal is made up of the favorite foods of individuals and the menus vary from year to year. Once we had black-eyed peas instead of our standard green beans. Another year it was derby pie and brussels sprouts.

Our son was eight years old when he drew turkey and dressing. After many tears he called the "turkey hotline": He found a succulent wild rice dressing recipe and rose at 6 A.M. to roast the turkey! He basked in compliments at dinner, saying, "That wasn't so hard." Younger children can use frozen bread dough or partially prepared foods like canned pie filling. Don't underestimate what children can do in the kitchen. In addition, there are many children's cookbooks or resources available with easy recipes that kids can do all by themselves.

Our family always uses our finest linen, china, and silverware. Even young children can make simple decorations to lend a festive air to the holiday meal.

Each family member serves the dish they prepare (an adult carves the turkey). There is only one rule: If anyone dislikes a dish, they must nevertheless encourage all efforts with enthusiastic compliments. (No "Oh, yucks!" allowed.)

Such a Thanksgiving dinner fosters fond memories. Since beginning this tradition several years ago, our grown daughters still anticipate "drawing for the dinner," and preparing a unique specialty.

Helen Meadows
Trout Creek, Montana

An Old-Fashioned Christmas

As a family we have interviewed older people in our community and pored over books to find out how Christmas was celebrated years ago.

Starting the first of December, we turn off our television and start using our free time to make homemade Christmas presents and decorations for our home and tree. Everything in our home connected with Christmas, or everything we give as gifts, has to be homemade.

Our tree, for example, has no electrical lights. We even used old-fashioned recipes to make cookies, candy, and our Christmas dinner.

Yes, you can survive as a family and have a wonderful Christmas without a TV, VCR, and all the electronic games!

Margaret B. Huff
Strong, Maine

Christmas Angels

If you've heard of secret pals, you know what it means to be a Christmas angel.

On the first of December our family members draw names to see who will be whose Christmas angel. All through the month we do nice things for that person, such as make their bed, leave happy notes, and give small gifts, handmade or otherwise. All you have to do is use your imagination!

On Christmas Eve we reveal our Christmas angels and exchange gifts. We have an annual birthday party for Jesus on this night and this event only adds to the celebration.

Rev. and Mrs. Terry Chapman
Moravia, Iowa

Straw in the Manger

Set up your nativity set and leave a pile of straw next to the empty manger. Whenever someone does a good deed he or she can secretly put in a piece of straw. The more good deeds done, the loftier and softer is Baby Jesus' bed when He is put into it on Christmas Eve.

Accompaniment to Advent

Every year our church plans a Sunday evening activity to make

Advent wreaths. The cost is minimal (the price of the metal wreath frames) and the fun and fellowship are beyond price.

Once the Advent season begins, every evening before dinner as a family we light the candles on the wreath. Afterward, we have a brief devotional with the focus on Jesus' birth and sing a Christmas carol. We sing all our favorites in the first weeks and then attempt to master new carols. Hopefully, some will find their way into our repertoire next year.

During Advent we also purchase an Advent calendar from our local Christian bookstore. Inside each window on the calendar is a Bible verse and the children take turns reading these throughout the holiday season. This activity is often combined with our dinner devotional and makes a wonderful family time.

Jackie White
Tippecanoe, Ohio

The Tree of Treats

In order to stretch out the Christmas treats and activities we like to share as a family, we utilize a posterboard-size Christmas tree, set up like an Advent calendar, with twenty-five little windows cut out for each day until Christmas.

To make the tree, proceed as follows. Cut two identical Christmas tree shapes, one from green posterboard and one from white posterboard; laminate each one separately. Cut twenty-five window flaps on the green tree, then align and glue it to the white tree, making sure not to glue the flaps shut. Using an erasable marker (so tree can be reused), write in a treat under each flap. Then, every morning during December, have the children open a window to see what their treat is for that day.

Some things we use as treats include activities that we traditionally do during the holidays or are related to the season, such as a school band concert, the community Christmas parade, our family caroling night, and holiday television specials. We also like to include activities that help to combat the busy scheduling that often occurs at this time. For example, we let a child pick one Christmas book for a parent to read aloud for the family; we plan a shopping trip to the dollar store for Mom or Dad's present; we bake cookies or wrap presents together. We also write in little gifts such as new socks, refills for the gumball machine, or new batteries for games that need them.

Cathie Orozco
College Station, Texas

An Ornament a Year

Each year sit down together as a family and make a special Christmas ornament to hang from the tree. It can be made from items bought in a craft store or from things that you have around the house. For example, use clothespins to make doll-like ornaments; glue glitter to plastic eggs and fill them with a small gift; cut out a star from cardboard and cover with aluminum foil. Use your imagination. Just make the ornament special to you and have a good time in the process. Over the years you will have quite a collection that will bring memories flooding back.

A Gift of Their Own

For many years, as we don't give allowances, we felt our sons were missing out on the experience of selecting special gifts for family members. We now give each child a certain amount of spending money with which to purchase Christmas presents.

What a wonderful experience it has been seeing them budget their money while coming up with some truly unique gifts! (As they get older and have individual sources of income, they will, of course,

be on their own.) They are learning not only the fundamentals of
family finance, but the joy of giving.

Mrs. Kenneth Long
Accident, Maryland

Goody Giving

To encourage our children in the joy of giving at Christmas, we
assemble goody bags. A few homemade cookies, candy, and a candy
cane make up our bags. When someone visits our home during the
holidays, the kids rush to present them with their goody gift. Everyone feels blessed.

Mila Rowe
Frankfort, Ohio

The Holiday *Herald?*

This Christmas make a mock family newspaper and include it with
your Christmas cards. Have everyone in the family submit their
favorite picture, story, or memory from that year.

Sandy Umber
Springdale, Arkansas

Respectfully Yours

Here's a neat and inexpensive gift idea...what you might call a gift
of respect. Write the following on a card and insert in a box or bag:

Here is a box of nothing. I am giving you a day where I ask nothing of you, and I do nothing to bother you.

Sandy Umber
Springdale, Arkansas

Happy Birthday, Jesus!

Our family has a birthday party for Jesus every year on Christmas Eve. Instead of giving traditional gifts, we pledge gifts of Christian service to be accomplished throughout the coming year. Children, perhaps with the help of a parent, also give such gifts, with the idea of definitely carrying them out. Ideas include tithing one's allowance, running errands for an elderly or physically or mentally challenged neighbor, being especially kind to children at school who are friendless, and living in harmony with one's siblings.

At the actual party we sing "Happy Birthday" to Jesus, we serve holiday cake and ice cream, and we read the Bible story of His foretold birth. Each family member takes a turn reading at least one verse. The living and dining rooms are bathed in light from our extensive holiday candle collection, reminiscent of the one true Light who came into our darkened world.

We often invite relatives and neighbors to join in the festivities, and then we extend an invitation to join us for the candlelight Christmas Eve service at our church.

Stacey Murphy
Newcomerstown, Ohio

The Proof Is in the Pudding?

On Christmas Eve our family enjoys having rice porridge or rice pudding. One whole almond is hidden in the bowl of pudding.

We eat and eat until one of us finds the special almond. He or she must show the others the whole almond unscathed. That lucky person then gets a gift of candy or some similar prize.

Ruth K. Molich
Paso Robles, California

Dinner by the Tree

After you and your family have spent hours decorating the tree, why not take time to enjoy your work. Set aside one night when everyone can be there and plan to have dinner by the tree. Turn on only the tree lights and sit back, eat, and admire what you've done. After dinner, sing your favorite Christmas carols.

Lights in the Darkness

Here's a Christmas tree lighting tradition that brings joy to our family and helps us to stay focused on the true meaning of this blessed holiday.

After a hot, home-cooked breakfast, we start out early in the morning for the country to cut down our tree. At least an hour is spent looking for that "perfect" tree (led by our oldest daughter). On the way home we stop for hot chocolate and take time to laugh and enjoy our tree-hunting experiences. Once home we set up the tree and spend the afternoon decorating. When supper is over we prepare for the tree lighting ceremony. All lights are off in the house.

We begin with this prayer: "Heavenly Father, You created trees. They are strong like Your love for us and are green and alive like Your Holy Spirit that is alive in us and helping us to grow. The lights and ornaments adorn our tree like the blessings You have given us, especially the blessing of Your Son Jesus who adorns our life today and forever. Bless this tree that we may enjoy its fragrance, lights, and beauty. May we find joy in Jesus. In the name of Jesus, Amen."

Someone then reads the Scripture selection, Luke 2:8-14.

We join in singing "O, Christmas Tree" and after the last stanza our middle daughter has the honor of turning on the tree lights. At this time the family exchanges homemade ornaments with each other.

Finally, we sing two favorite Christmas carols, "Joy to the World" and "Silent Night," and have a short benediction.

The Miller Family
Canton, Michigan

A Stocking for Baby Jesus

When hanging the family Christmas stockings, add one for the Baby Jesus and have each member of the family insert a special gift. It could be a promise to be kinder to others or to donate to a local charity. Whatever your heart says to you—something that is meaningful to both you and the Lord—should be considered.

An International Holiday

Looking for new ideas for celebrating Christmas? Adopt the traditions of a new country each year. One year celebrate Christmas the French way, another year follow the Dutch ways, and so on. Begin your research early and find out what foods, customs, and decorations are used in the different countries of the world at Christmastime and incorporate them into your celebrations.

Guess the Gift

If you have the time, slow down the gift-opening process and watch each other's reactions as the gifts are opened. The recipient (and the giver) has time to savor the new gift, and your children learn self-control. Make the process more fun by attaching a rhyme or poem that gives clues to the identity of the gift. Everyone then tries to guess what the gift is before it is opened.

A Special Tablecloth

Use this cloth only at Christmas and make it to fit a table other than the dinner table (it will be difficult to clean). Cut red, green, or white felt to a size appropriate for the table. From other pieces of felt, cut out various ornament shapes, such as stars, circles, diamonds, candycanes, and so on and decorate them with sequins, beads, buttons, and glitter (use glue or sew them on). Glue or sew the "ornaments" to the tablecloth. The cloth can be completed in one year or done a bit at a time over the years.

Sign Right Here!

Make or buy a special mantel cloth to be used above the fireplace or on a table during the holidays. Before, during, or after dinner have each guest sign his or her name on the cloth. Later, embroider over their signatures and add the date next to each. Besides having a permanent record of who was at each of your celebrations, the sight of the mantel cloth will bring back all those wonderful memories of the fun times you and your family had together.

Keep the Christmas Spirit Alive

Do you know some people who pack away all the Christmas trimmings on the day after Christmas? They take down the tree, turn off the music, and throw the cards in the trash. But wait, don't throw those cards away!

Here's a tradition that children love. After Christmas we put all the cards in a basket and each day we take turns selecting a card during our family devotions.

We then spend a special time in prayer for the family who sent us that card. In fact, we might even jot them a note or give them a call. Christmas is an attitude of the heart and children need to know that the Christmas spirit can be kept alive all year.

Annette Aycock
Florence, South Carolina

Hats Off to You

Every New Year's Eve our family has a hat contest.

We gather together an assortment of such things as paper bags, newspapers, feathers, bows, ribbons, colored paper, doilies, paper plates, paper cups, scissors, paste, string, yarn, and rubber bands. Each family member then designs and makes a hat to wear.

The hats are planned and constructed amid much secrecy and hilarious laughter. When at last finished, we model our hats and vote for the one we like best. Then, with hats still on our heads, we parade around the house—or around the block if we are brave— with the creator of the winning *chapeau* in the lead!

Lois Rehder Holmes
Havana, Illinois

Bags of Gifts

Ever since my husband and I were married, we have had a special way of bringing in the new year. Our boys, who are now seven and ten, thoroughly enjoy this tradition and look forward to it each year.

On New Year's Eve each person is given a brown grocery bag to decorate any way they like. When done, we look at all the bags to see each person's ideas, then line them up in the living room and fill them with small, inexpensive wrapped gifts. Some examples of what we give are Christmas decorations and candy, which we buy at half-price, and little toys and gadgets that we have accumulated throughout the year. We usually have a few extra people who stay overnight with us on New Year's Eve, so they participate also. On New Year's Day the boys wake us up and we all open our bags; the youngest person is first.

Celeste Boyer
Wannaska, Minnesota

What a Year!

For the last few years we have kept a large planning calendar near the telephone in our kitchen. Every time one or all of our family enjoys a special activity (going to a play, sleeping over at a friend's, an award or ceremony, visiting Grandma, and so on) it is recorded in special colors on the calendar.

On New Year's Eve, as we retire our calendar for the next year's, we leaf through the months, remembering our favorite fun times. Our family is always amazed at how many we've forgotten. Yet as the blessing of memories returns to us, our year is ended on a note of thankfulness for the chance to share them all over again, together.

Anne Calodich Fone
Tillson, New York

The Book of Family Fun

travel

———

God has provided us with lessons
of the world and of life. . .
whether we travel one mile or one thousand.

———

Before You Go...

...check out the area you will be visiting for places that appeal to your individual interests. Many are free or inexpensive.

For instance, our daughter has always loved horses and is curious about the different breeds. By writing to various horse breeders before our visit, we were invited to tour some fabulous ranches hosted by outgoing, hospitable people. These visits were free, and, on occasion, our children were even allowed to ride the horses!

Another time we visited the home of a famous author whose books we had enjoyed. Our daughter had been corresponding with him a short time. This was a memorable event: The author was gracious enough to allow photos, and he also presented our daughter with the gift of a beautiful hardbound book.

Planning such special outings gives children a chance to develop confidence and letter-writing skills. In addition, we all get to meet new people and learn about each other's interests.

Janet Lee Friesorger
Pinconning, Michigan

FYI: The Chamber of Commerce

Before we go on vacation, or just somewhere new for the weekend, I always call or write the local Chamber of Commerce.

For little or no charge the Chamber of Commerce will send you all kinds of tourist information. Places to go and see, things to do, a calendar of events, and sometimes even a map are included. This way you can pick out things to do ahead of time and look forward even more to your upcoming adventure.

For the address and telephone number of any Chamber of Commerce in the United States, simply call your local chapter and they will be happy to look it up for you.

Kendy Moore
Merlin, Oregon

Traveling Jitters

Don't let the fear of the unknown stop you from making memories with your children. I know the feeling as I live 2,000 miles from my home and was hesitant about making such a trip without my husband. What if someone grabbed one of the children in an airport terminal?

The trip home, however, was fabulous. My travel agent planned an itinerary with no long waits. I put on my I-know-where-I'm-going face and marched through the terminals unhindered. Stewardesses were very helpful and so were other passengers. Such a stress-free experience has made us all into better travelers.

Terry L. Pfleghaar
Elk River, Minnesota

─────

Have Travel Tote, Will Go

Here's a travel tip that my daughter (the mother of seven children) is continuing in her family.

Whenever we traveled out of state, I always provided each child with a durable tote bag containing tape, scissors, scrapbook, paper, pencils, and a map. The children would follow the maps and gather souvenirs at stops to place in their scrapbooks. Not only did the children learn to read maps, they also cared for their own things and (there's more) kept interested in the trip. Three words rarely spoken were "How much longer?"

Twenty years later, the now grown-up children still enjoy looking at their travel scrapbooks.

Janet Sliwoski
Shelbyville, Michigan

[Editors' note: Try finding boxes (maybe empty cereal boxes, sturdy department store boxes, and so on) to sit on top of carseats and to lay on a child's lap. Fill the boxes with craft supplies before each trip.]

Breaking Up a Long Trip

When we visit my family—a fourteen-hour trip from our house—I plan ahead to make it a real adventure.

On scraps of paper I write an assortment of trip ideas and goodies and place slips in a paper bag. Every hour one child is allowed to draw one slip of paper and see what the surprise will be for the group.

Who knows what will be next? It might be a car game, candy bars, a cassette tape, or magazines. We might all have to sing songs! These activities help ease the passage of time as the children eagerly anticipate when it's time for the next drawing and what it will be.

Phyllis Moore D'Amico
Clifton Park, New York

The Ice Cream Kit

Our family of seven loved to eat ice cream and we spent much time traveling in the car. In order to combine these two favorite activities in an affordable way, we didn't go anywhere without our "ice cream kit." Our kit consisted of Dad's old metal lunch box, seven styrofoam cups, seven spoons, an ice cream scoop, and something for cleaning sticky fingers.

Along our most traveled routes we had our favorite grocery stores that carried the widest variety of ice cream flavors. On a rotating basis one of us would go with Dad into the store to choose the flavor of the half-gallon of ice cream that he would buy for us to share.

Mom had the job of scooping the ice cream and packing it firmly into each of the cups. Dad always got his first and it was piled high so he could eat as much as possible without a spoon while he was driving. By the time Mom got all five kids' cups dished out, Dad was always ready for seconds. The kids were ready for seconds soon after that.

When we had friends along, we'd sometimes buy a whole gallon of ice cream but it was difficult to get it all eaten before it melted. Our friends would comment, "Yeah, I like ice cream but not that much at one time." However, when a half-gallon had to be divided more than seven ways, there just wasn't enough to go around.

One evening all the kids were sleeping in the back seat. Dad whispered to Mom, "Do you think we should stop for some...?" and my three-year-old sister sat right up and said, "Ice cream? Where?"

After each use, the ice cream kit was brought in, utensils washed and cups replaced so it was ready for our next trip. This was one item that we rarely forgot to pack. I can hardly wait until my own family is big enough to have an ice cream kit of our own! We have only a few more years to wait.

Ruth Weyers
Canton, Illinois

Snack Packs

Since our family travels frequently, we have found ways to cut costs and eliminate unnecessary stops. Each morning I pack lunches and ample snacks and drinks for each family member. Each person has their own minicooler for the day. With the little coolers positioned next to each person in the car, people eat whenever they want.

Claudia Cushen Pinkston
Lexington, South Carolina

―――――

A Notebook to Go

A travel notebook is a worthy activity for elementary school children. Buy a looseleaf notebook, dividers, paper (lined and unlined), and pencils and markers. One way to organize such a trip record would be as follows:

1. *Interesting facts:* Before the trip have the child do a little research on one particular destination of the upcoming trip. Be sure to include a brief history and places of interest to the child.

2. *Travel log:* Leave plenty of paper in this section for a diary of the trip.

3. *Postcards:* The unlined paper in this section is ready for pasting in postcards accumulated during the trip.

4. *Quiet time:* The child can record special verses or prayer requests each day. What has the child noticed about God's magnificent world that surprised him or her?

5. *Money:* It's a good idea to keep an account of your trip money and what it was used to buy. See how quickly it disappears!

6. The final section should be blank pages for trip saver games, drawing pictures, and whatever else sounds fun.

*Adapted from **The Big Book of Family Fun** by Claudia Arp and Linda Dillow (Thomas Nelson Publishers, 1994). Used with permission by the publisher.*

The Perfect Car Trip

When traveling with preteens and teens, they can be given the responsibility of loading the car, registering at motels, paying for food and lodging, pumping and paying for gasoline, and recording all expenses and mileage. Adults should, of course, serve as advisors at all times.

Before the trip begins, age-appropriate activities include planning sightseeing detours by reading travel brochures or library reference books covering the regions included in the trip plans. At each stop, children can gather an assortment of free brochures and buy postcards to be filed away later for school projects or hung as mobiles.

When in the car, an ice chest in the back seat makes a neat seat divider when covered with a beach towel. Each child then has his or her defined "turf" with no fighting about space. The chest also becomes a table for travel games.

Elizabeth Garvey
Howell, Michigan

Every Trip Needs a Navigator

After our auto club provides us with the "trip ticket," my husband highlights the route on our atlas. Our sons then alternate as navigator and comfort coordinator.

The navigator keeps the map and is responsible for assuring that the driver stays on the proper route. He lets the driver know which cities and landmarks should be coming up and advises the driver on the speed limit. In addition, he keeps the driver informed on traffic conditions. The navigator feels pretty important!

The comfort coordinator changes the cassette/radio station and, as necessary, sees to the comfort of the driver and the other passengers.

Such knowledge of the road has become invaluable to our sons as they have grown older.

The Reed Family
Hinesville, Georgia

Count the Smiles

Whoever said that the journey should be as fun as arriving at the destination didn't have to ride six hours in a van with four small children. Parents to the rescue!

Before we leave home I make a small chart to represent how long our trip will be. I draw a small circle for each thirty-minute segment of the trip. On a six-hour trip to Grandmom's, for example, I would have drawn twelve circles.

Once we leave, I post the chart and set a timer for thirty minutes. When the timer goes off, we put a "smiley face" in one of the circles and reset the clock. At the end of each time period we also take something from a premade goody bag. Items include a cassette, gum, puppets, taffy, a devotional, flash cards, writing paper, a craft, coloring books, long-lasting lollipops, and so on.

You never again have to hear "How much longer?" The answer is obvious: "Only three more smiley faces 'til Grandmom's!"

Annette Aycock
Florence, South Carolina

Half the Fun Is Getting There!

Our family prayerfully added the above attitude to our adventures years ago, and what a difference those words have made!

Before we embark on a new adventure, as a family we listen to family and friends' recommendations of places to visit; we peruse travel books and watch travel videos from the library or from Christian publishers; and we investigate the travel section in newspapers.

While we have an ultimate destination in mind, we enjoy meeting and watching people along the way and at the same time taking advantage of new sights. We witness wherever the Lord may lead us, making sure to leave Christian tracts in restrooms, as an extra tip in restaurants, and in telephone booths. Another way to witness is to send postcards to friends with a Scripture or words of praise. These cards have the potential to bless many postal workers as well as the recipients. Be sure to send yourself a postcard, too, complete with date and postmark!

One Sunday an advertisement in a newspaper seized our attention: "Beautiful Scenic Lakes, No Crowds, Discount Prices." We called the toll-free number and, to make the story short, embarked later on our next family adventure...houseboating!

Traffic to and from Lake Mohave, Arizona, was minimal as this was the off season. Although we had never gone houseboating before, we needed little orientation as we had had some boating experience. In only a matter of minutes we were on the water.

All three of us took turns navigating, cooking and cleaning, and selecting family activities. We also had plenty of time for fishing, reading and writing, and soaking up the sun. Family devotions took on a special beauty against a background of miles of beaches, small hills, and clear sky and water. This minivacation remains one of our special blessings, best bargains, and favorite memories.

Larry W. and Suanne Shankle Jones
Canton, Ohio

Take Six at the Swings?

One of the best ways we have found to relieve boredom on long car trips is to stop at community playgrounds. We get off the highway and take a drive around, keeping our eyes on the lookout for such an area. (Of course, you could stop and ask someone if you don't want to spend time looking, but part of the fun is to see who can spot a playground first. An added benefit is seeing some interesting local sights you otherwise might have missed.)

An hour spent playing in the fresh air, usually including a snack or a picnic lunch, revives our spirits for yet another long stretch in the car. And it doesn't cost a thing.

Nancy Van Cott
New Milford, Pennsylvania

Down the Road a Spell

Traveling a great many miles can be tiring to children and, consequently, to parents. One solution: Look into interesting places to visit close to home and then pursue the activities your family enjoys.

When our children were small we found a town twenty miles from where we lived that fit the bill. On one outing we started with a picnic breakfast in a park. During the day we would choose to visit one of many museums or perhaps go to a stable and ride the trails. When the day was over, we knew it was only a short drive back home.

Here's a hint to keep track of several children: Dress them alike. I made simple summer tops for the girls and shirts for the boys out of the same material. At a moment's glance you know whose children are yours, even if they have their backs to you. Others will also recognize that they belong together.

Janice Ruoff
Helena, Missouri

In the Victorian Age

Tours of Victorian-age homes in our area are inexpensive—free or less than one dollar per person—and offer a hands-on experience of times past. The children have a great deal of fun as well.

As a learning experience, we were told the difference between a restoration and a preservation. In one home that was once owned by a family that had nine children, the tour guide geared the entire tour to my children. The guide described how Victorian children would be dressed and she instructed my two on how proper Victorian children behaved. From that moment on, they walked with their chins held high and backs erect!

When the tour was over, my children knew all about the "ice man" and how Victorian children learned table manners. Such information can only reinforce what we've been teaching them at home!

Mary Jo Zimmerly
Greenwood, Indiana

Indiana Calls Me

One summer our family decided the most economical and interesting place for us to vacation was in our own home state of Indiana.

Our first stop was the home of author and naturalist, Gene Straton Porter. Our children had seen the movie, "Girl of the Limberlost," and were familiar with Porter's interest in moths. We then toured the home of Levi Coffin, a Quaker man known for his involvement with the underground railroad. Our children thoroughly enjoyed "meeting" these people and exploring their homes. In addition, we visited an Indian mound and spent time exploring one of Indiana's many caves.

Since we were not in a hurry, we chose to take the scenic route and traveled country roads and small highways. We browsed through antique shops along the way and were also able to experience nature close up. Many times we stopped to pick wildflowers, and one time a fawn even stopped beside the road so that we could take its picture. We took along the *Audubon Society Field Guide* books on North American trees and butterflies and these were excellent resources.

After each day of sightseeing, we enjoyed a nice, cool swim in a modern motel pool...a wonderful way to end the day.

Jennifer Canady
Logansport, Indiana

Your House or Mine?

If you have friends or family who live far away, you may want to consider swapping homes for a low-cost vacation.

Remember to leave your home clean and the refrigerator full before departing for your home away from home. Such courtesies ensure that your guests will be comfortable, and will have more money to spend on entertainment than on food.

Staying in someone's home also means your family will feel more a part of their new surroundings and will really get the flavor of a new part of the country. Swapping homes is an educational, fun, and relaxing way to travel!

Melissa Dillman
Middleburg, Pennsylvania

A Camper to Go!

In celebration of paying off our home mortgage, we took our first real vacation in twenty years. (According to our teenagers, a real vacation is when you don't visit relatives!)

We purchased a used pop-up camper, which we sold after the trip for exactly the costs we put into it. Also, we prepared enough food so that only two meals and a few miscellaneous groceries were purchased on the trip. So far, so good!

After our three teenagers got off work, we headed out on our adventure. With five drivers we could easily drive all night and sleep in comfort in the reclining chairs of our van. For the next six days we pushed on, covering over 3,600 miles through eleven states!

We enjoyed and marveled at the unpopulated miles of Wyoming and Montana. Our itinerary included the Badlands of South Dakota; Mount Rushmore and Rushmore Cave, South Dakota; Wheat-Montana Farms, Montana; Yellowstone National Park and Grand Teton National Park, Wyoming; Chimney Rock and Omaha Zoo, Nebraska.

We praised God for a safe and enjoyable trip that cost under $500 (not including two van tires).

Janet Yoder
Goshen, Indiana

The Beauty of It All

We enjoy taking short minivacations. A drive up to the mountains is always invigorating and a renewal for the soul. There is such beauty to behold in the open country. To help the children appreciate what God has given us, we play a little game while we are out hiking. Each person finds something to thank the Father for, such as a small colorful stone, a towering tree, or even a majestic hawk soaring above. All of us soon find the beauty in even the smallest things.

Lisa D. Hughes
Phoenix, Arizona

When Travel's a Treat

Instead of trick or treating, every year we treat ourselves to a trip on Halloween night. Our destination: Hueston Woods Lodge, a local state park.

We pack a change of clothes, pajamas, and swimsuits and leave as early as possible or right after school. We pick up Grandma (she's lots of fun) and drive about an hour to this beautiful lodge. After we check in we go for a swim in the indoor pool and later enjoy a special dinner in front of a fireplace in the lodge's lovely restaurant. There's always time for another swim after dinner and then it's back to the room to read, play games, and eat snacks. The next morning we treat ourselves (again!) to a big breakfast, reading, and enjoying a view of the lake.

Autumn is such a beautiful time for a ride in the country...and the start of a wonderful family tradition.

Sue Bevin
Norwood, Ohio

In Praise of National Parks

A vacation in a national park is always an adventure. Our children keep their eyes peeled toward the woods and fields as we drive through or hike, anticipating rare views of wildlife. Nowhere else on earth can you gaze at such awe-inspiring landscapes and be so close to such a variety of animals.

When we go, we enjoy hiking to magnificent waterfalls, and then partaking of delicious picnic lunches! Such a vacation is certainly economical as we save money on meals and the cost of camping in the national parks is very reasonable.

Our most rewarding trip was to Yellowstone National Park. There we witnessed geysers, large herds of buffalo, a cow moose with her calf, and a big bull elk. Talk about a thrill!

Arlene King
Philadelphia, Mississippi

Hands-on Fun at Edwards Air Force Base

Whether as the sole destination for a quick getaway or a thoroughly entertaining and educational stopover on the way to one of the three national parks nearby, the annual Edwards Air Force Base (EAFB) open house is a hit with our family.

Located southeast of Bakersfield and north of San Fernando, California, EAFB is the home of the Air Force Test Flight Center. The machinery displayed portrays exciting excerpts from twentieth-century aviation history, from early mach-busters to the space shuttles of NASA. The hands-on exhibits are designed to be kid-friendly: Our daughters have climbed in and out of cockpits and sat inside a real M1 Abrams main battle tank. Throughout the day high performance aircraft roar and zoom overhead in daring maneuvers and close formations. After flying, pilots are readily available for autographs and to pose for photographs. Our girls have even walked right up to Chuck Yeager, who gladly signed their programs. You never know who will be at Edwards!

With over 300,000 visitors attending this *free* event, we avoid traffic by arriving ninety minutes before the gate opens at 8 A.M. The show itself starts an hour later and ends at 4 P.M. While most of the crowd is still waiting to get in, we've already toured the museum and visitor's center. By 2 P.M. we've seen everything, met everyone, and are ready to leave hours before the closing rush. Food vendors are available or you can pack a picnic. The average temperature during October is a pleasant 70 degrees Fahrenheit.

For further information and the exact date of this year's open house, call EAFB Public Relations at (805) 277-1110. For hotel information, send $3 to the Lancaster Chamber of Commerce, 44335

Lowtree Ave., Lancaster, California 93534.

Debra L. Lewis
Longmont, Colorado

Fun on the Oregon Trail

After my daughters read *Little House on the Prairie* and other titles by Laura Ingalls Wilder, they tried to imagine life without VCRs, ATMs, and indoor plumbing.

Taking full advantage of their interest, I planned a quick overnight trip to Independence Rock on the Oregon Trail near Casper, Wyoming. To re-create the feel of the pioneers who traveled in covered wagons, we set some radical ground rules before departing: No radio and no air conditioning in the car. We might not have to face dysentery or burned skin from the dust kicked up by oxen along the way, but choosing not to use the air conditioning in August took a great deal of courage!

It was worth it. No gaudy road signs reminded us how far we had to go. Like the original pioneers, we simply had to look for the rock, and it wasn't hard to find. We pulled into the well-kept rest area and parked. Before climbing the rock we spent several minutes studying the displays posted at the entrance to the Trail. We could easily see where wagon trains had circled and camped. The girls scaled the rock in no time and began seaching for the oldest signatures they could find. Many were carved over 100 years ago!

That night we stayed in a nice hotel in Casper and played board games, told wild stories, and read more about the history of the Oregon Trail. For accommodation and restaurant information, write or call the Chamber of Commerce, 500 N. Central, P.O. Box 399, Casper, Wyoming 82602; (307) 234-5311.

Debra L. Lewis
Longmont, Colorado

Vacation at Home

If you can't go away for a vacation, have one around your home. Plan day trips to special places and *do not let any work get in your way.* If you have an answering machine, make use of it as much as possible. Be sure you're out of the house right after breakfast and don't come home until bedtime.

Go to the parks, beaches, museums, and other interesting places in your area; spend the day at an amusement park. When you're done with that, go to a concert, play, or the movies. Stay within an easy driving range of home so that you are not too tired to enjoy yourself when you arrive at your destination. Remember that the important thing is to relax and enjoy your time together.

A Time in Haiti

One year when my husband's parents were missionaries to Haiti, as were my brother and sister-in-law, our family decided to spend Christmas with them. No family vacation before or since has been as meaningful or exciting as that adventure.

We had the usual fun times while there, enjoying tree trimming, caroling, and attending a nativity reenactment. A five-day camping experience in the mountains near the border of the Dominican Republic was also memorable. However, the single most outstanding memory for all of us happened on Christmas Day when we took homemade popcorn balls and shared in a joyful celebration with a group of Haitian people that lived in a tiny village nearby.

Though by our standards they were destitute, and by their physical appearance most of them looked malnourished, the thrill of watching them play simple games, listen attentively to the Christmas story, then hearing their thanks for our popcorn gift was beyond words. For many days and weeks afterward our sons were deeply affected by what they had seen and felt. Such an experience has shaped much of their perspective even now as young men preparing for their life's work.

Brenda Picazo
Springville, New York

Fun-Time Education

by Norene Morris

My husband Paul's mind was always consumed by numbers. By the time I would finish presenting a problem, he had already calculated the solution in his head. Our children inherited his mathematical aptitude.

I think immediately of car games. Car riding for our children was "fun time" because whenever we climbed into the car the children continued their game of counting license plates. Each New Year's Day when the new license plates came out, the game began anew.

First, everyone had to look for a number 1 all by itself, or separated from other numbers on a license plate. The first 1 found was the starting gun for the new year. No matter who found it, it was everyone's property; looking for 2, however, everyone was on their own. Competition was high to see who could keep ahead. Dad usually did and our children said he got the jump on them driving to work. He grinned at them and said, "Well, when you start driving to work, you'll join my league." That ended the matter.

A side benefit we didn't count on was how very conscious the children became of cars as they crossed streets or played outside. Each year a new starting number was chosen by the children. Fifty?

One hundred? One year our young son shouted out, "Ninety-nine!" That was as high as he could count, but we started with 99 anyway.

When Dad sensed license hunting had lost its appeal, he started another game. "What is 2 times 2, plus 2, divided by 3, plus 1, plus 5, minus 2, plus 10?" Foreheads were furrowed and you could almost hear the mental wheels turning. As the children grew older and became more math-proficient, the problems grew longer and more complicated and were dictated faster. The growth of quick figuring soon showed up when our children went shopping with us. Their math grades in school also improved.

The car wasn't our only playground. To put a check on the dinner table eat-and-run idea, we began playing "Rhyme." Most of our games we played were made up and sometimes the rules changed as we went along.

"Rhyme" popped up on its own at dinner one night when one of the children happened to ask for something on the table and it came out in rhyme. We all laughed, which encouraged the next rhyme, and then it graduated into a real game. Comments like "For goodness sake, please pass the cake" or "Pass me a spoon, can't sit here 'til noon" were bandied about. Here's another: "Do I have to sit? Mom, I gotta git." You get the drift. The big plus of this game was the increase in word knowledge and vocabulary, both for the children and Mom and Dad.

Every so often some mood coaxed our family into talking about "the olden days" when Mom and Dad were kids. "How old were you, Dad, when you got your two-wheeler bike?" our son asked. Our oldest daughter of eleven questioned, "Mom, how old were you when you began wearing silk stockings?" These were glad open-door times to pass on our heritage.

Games popped up according to interest. No matter how simple, there was never a put-down of anyone. Our children grew to converse and express their opinions with us, each other, and eventually other people, unafraid. And I don't think (?) they realized Mom and Dad snuck in some lessons on manners along the way.

Modern parents, hang in there! Our grandchildren delightedly fall into the same tactics when they come to visit Grandma and Grandpa.

Copyright © 1995 by Norene Morris.
Norene Morris enjoys writing historical inspirational
romances and playing with her grandchildren.

Car Logo Bingo

When you see a car logo that is on your particular bingo card of car logos, mark through that square. The first player to get all the logos down, across, or diagonal, wins. If you aren't sure about an emblem, refer to the Logo Pool that follows.

Logo Pool

Taken from My Anytime Anyplace Activity Book
by W. B. Freeman (Thomas Nelson Publishers, 1994).
Used with permission by the publisher.

I Spy Tic-Tac-Toe

Game boards for this game should be made ahead of time to save
confusion. Make a square much like one for tic-tac-toe only larger

and draw in each space a common sight on a trip. Examples include a familiar fast-food restaurant, a bicycle, a bus stop, a church, a taxi cab, a speed limit sign, a camera, a familiar hotel chain, an airplane, and so on.

Two players may play and each requires a pencil. One player will be the X and the other will be the O. X will spy on the left side of the street or highway and O will spy on the right side. When a player sees an object outside that matches one on the game board, he or she names it and puts an X or O on the picture. A box can only have one X or O in it. The player who marks three boxes in a row, column, or diagonally, wins.

Adapted from My Anytime Anyplace Activity Book
by W. B. Freeman *(Thomas Nelson Publishers, 1994).*
Used with permission by the publisher.

License Plate Plus

All you need is a pencil and pad of paper and cars on a highway. First, write down the numbers on the license plates of the next twenty cars that you pass. Then add them up. For example, if the license plate were of a single car 8EX 234, the total for that plate would be 17.

Now write down the license plate numbers of the next twenty cars that pass you. Add these numbers. Which total is greater?

Adapted from My Anytime Anyplace Activity Book
by W. B. Freeman *(Thomas Nelson Publishers, 1994).*
Used with permission by the publisher.

Travel "Standby"

Here's another trip saver, and one that has passed the test of time.

As you gaze out the window, try locating something that starts with the letter *A*; go on then to the letters *B*, *C*, and so on until you reach the end of the alphabet. Once you find your letter, call out your answer. No two people can have the same answer for a letter. If you can't find a certain letter, you are out of the game (or silent for a long time).

Stacy Miller
Kokomo, Indiana

Words In a Word

Take a phrase and see how many different words can be made from its letters. See who can come up with the most words, the longest words, the funniest words, and so on. Use biblical locations and personalities such as "Mediterranean maelstrom" (Paul's journey), "Babylonian behemoth," "Nebuchadnezzar's neuroses," and so on.

Adapted from My Anytime Anyplace Activity Book
by W. B. Freeman (Thomas Nelson Publishers, 1994).
Used with permission by the publisher.

Oxymorons and Palindromes

Here's an activity for your older children, but you are sure to find it challenging as well.

An *oxymoron*, lest we forget, is the combination of two words that expresses contradictory ideas. A *palindrome* is a word or phrase that reads the same backward and forward. Here are some examples of oxymorons and palindromes but the real test is whether the kids can create some themselves. Our family uses words from our trip and develops oxymorons and palindromes around them.

Oxymorons: Sweet sorrow
                Jumbo shrimp
                Winter sports (to *some* people!)

Palindromes: Name no one man.
                Madam, I'm Adam.

Judy Clum
Tuscarawas, Ohio

A Battle of Thumbs

All right, this one can get out of hand, but kids still love to thumb wrestle.

In case it's been a while, here's how the game works. Two players grip hands and then, to begin, touch thumbs to the opposite sides of each other's thumb three times before the wrestling commences. The winner must hold the other person's thumb down for a count of three seconds using only his or her thumb.

Children close in age are, of course, the worthiest opponents but parents and children can play together if the adults give themselves some sort of handicap. Our family plays this in the car, on the plane, and even waiting for our food in a restaurant.

Ellen Caughey
Harrington Park, New Jersey

This Trip Saver's a Life Saver

On short car trips I devised a game called "Life Saver Races." It requires only the forethought of packing a roll or two of Life Savers.

197

Everyone begins with one Life Saver in his or her mouth. Whoever keeps his or her candy intact the longest, wins...and the prize is, of course, an extra Life Saver. The secret of winning is not to talk, which may make the trip much more pleasant.

My most talkative child (of eight children) holds the family record: He made one Life Saver last seven and a half miles!

Joan Lichter
Storm Lake, Iowa

The Long Road Home (and other stories)

To keep a crowded car situation under control, I made up two characters named Buster and Pomeroy and then I spun yarns about their adventures.

Buster lived on a ranch in Wyoming. I had visited such a ranch when I was ten and my memories gave me my setting. Pomeroy was a city boy whose parents went on a long trip abroad and who has come to live with relatives on the ranch. During one of the first episodes, Buster broke his leg and Pomeroy was forced to learn quickly about outdoor life on the ranch.

My children wanted me to tell the same story over each time, but I couldn't remember what had happened, so each trip meant a new story. I kept my voice low and the children remained quiet to listen. Even their father was interested in what would happen next!

One well-kept secret: My oldest daughter always wondered how I managed to end the stories just as we turned in the gate at home. It has something to do with the number of "very, verys" thrown in!

Joan Lichter
Storm Lake, Iowa

Contributors

199

Notes

Notes

Notes

Notes

Notes

Notes

Notes

Notes

Notes

Notes